Principles of Dramaturgy

In *Principles of Dramaturgy*, Robert Scanlan explains the invariant principles behind the construction of stage and performance events of any style or modality.

This book contains all that is essential for training a professional stage director and/or dramaturg, including the "plot-bead" technique for analyzing play scripts developed by Scanlan. It details all the steps for the full implementation of "Production Dramaturgy" as it is practiced in professional theatres, and treats *form* and *action* as foundational cornerstones of all performance, rather than "story" elements – a frequent and debilitating misprision in theatre practice. Scanlan's unique approach offers practical training that is supported by detailed diagrams and contextualized instructions, making this the missing text for classes in dramaturgy.

Serving stage directors, dramaturgs, actors, designers, and playwrights, *Principles of Dramaturgy* is a comprehensive guide that puts the training of capable practitioners above all else.

Robert Scanlan is a theatre director and Artistic Director of The Poets' Theatre. He has been teaching at Harvard University since 1989, first as the Literary Director of the American Repertory Theatre, where he headed the Dramaturgy and Playwriting Programs of the Institute for Advanced Theatre Training at Harvard. He later became Professor of the Practice of Theatre in the Department of English and chaired Harvard's Committee on Dramatics.

Focus on Dramaturgy
Series Editor: Magda Romanska

The *Focus on Dramaturgy* series from Routledge – developed in collaboration with TheTheatreTimes.com – is devoted to the craft of dramaturgy from multiple contemporary perspectives. This groundbreaking comprehensive series is authored by top professionals in the field, addressing a variety of current hot topics in dramaturgy.

The series is edited by Magda Romanska, an author of the critically-acclaimed *Routledge Companion to Dramaturgy*, dramaturg, writer, theatre scholar, and Editor-in-Chief of TheTheatreTimes.com.

Shakespeare in Three Dimensions
The Dramaturgy of *Macbeth* and *Romeo and Juliet*
Robert Blacker

Words for the Theatre
David Cole

Principles of Dramaturgy
Robert Scanlan

New Dramaturgies
Strategies and Exercises for 21st Century Playwriting
Mark Bly

For more information about this series, please visit:
www.routledge.com/performance/series/RFOD

Principles of Dramaturgy

Robert Scanlan

Routledge
Taylor & Francis Group
LONDON AND NEW YORK

First published 2020
by Routledge
2 Park Square, Milton Park, Abingdon, Oxon OX14 4RN

and by Routledge
605 Third Avenue, New York, NY 10017

First issued in paperback 2021

Routledge is an imprint of the Taylor & Francis Group, an informa business

© 2020 Robert Scanlan

Publisher's Note
The publisher has gone to great lengths to ensure the quality of
this reprint but points out that some imperfections in the
original copies may be apparent.

British Library Cataloguing-in-Publication Data
A catalogue record for this book is available from the British Library

Library of Congress Cataloging-in-Publication Data
Names: Scanlan, Robert, 1948– author.
Title: Principles of dramaturgy / Robert Scanlan.
Description: Abingdon, Oxon ; New York, NY : Routledge, 2019. |
Series: Focus on dramaturgy | Includes bibliographical references
and index.
Identifiers: LCCN 2019013174| ISBN 9781138071162 (hardback :
alk. paper) | ISBN 9781315114781 (ebook)
Subjects: LCSH: Theater–Production and direction. | Dramaturges.
Classification: LCC PN2053 .S2556 2019 | DDC 792.02/33–dc23
LC record available at https://lccn.loc.gov/2019013174

ISBN 13: 978-1-03-209147-1 (pbk)
ISBN 13: 978-1-138-07116-2 (hbk)

Typeset in Times New Roman
by Wearset Ltd, Boldon, Tyne and Wear

This book is dedicated to Joanne Baldine
and to our son, Robert

Contents

List of figures		viii
Preface		ix
Acknowledgments		xvi
	Introduction: what is dramaturgy?	1
1	Form	13
2	Action	49
3	Production Dramaturgy	72
	Afterword: some closing thoughts for playwrights	108
	Index	110

Figures

I.1 Example plot-bead diagrams – Samuel Beckett's *Rough for Theatre II* and Henrik Ibsen's *When We Dead Awaken*, Act II   4

1.1 Rough-hewn megalith of quarried marble and Michelangelo's David   15

1.2 Two of Michelangelo's "Captive Slaves"   16

1.3 Plot-bead diagram of Henrik Ibsen's *When We Dead Awaken*   25

1.4 Plot-bead diagram of Shakespeare's *Julius Caesar* Act IV, Scenes ii–iii   29

1.5 Detailed plot-bead diagram of the "Dead of Night" Coda, *Julius Caesar* Act IV, Scene iii   33

1.6 Basic plot-bead diagram of Robert Wilson's *Einstein on the Beach*   37

1.7 Robert Wilson's storyboard sketch for *Einstein on the Beach*   38

1.8 Plot-bead diagram of Samuel Beckett's *Rough for Theatre II*   42

2.1 Anthropomorphic spheres of action   67

3.1 Plot-bead diagram of Eugène Ionesco's *The Bald Soprano*   85

3.2a Rough-cut plot-bead diagram of Gotthold Lessing's *Minna von Barnhelm*, Act I   88

3.2b More structured plot-bead diagram of Act I of *Minna von Barnhelm*   89

Preface

This book is pragmatic and aimed at earnest students: it seeks to set forth principles that are essential in writing, staging, rehearsing, and performing plays. My own "plot-bead" diagrams, for instance (and instructions for how to use them), have found wide circulation and are in use wherever my former students are teaching or practicing in the theatre. I wish I had named them something more elegant – in Spanish, they are known more poetically as *diagramas de cuentas* – but their utility has spread their use, and theatre practitioners have long since heard of them. If plot-bead diagrams become *only* a method of play analysis, something has been lost, for they diagram something more mysterious and philosophical than may at first meet the eye. The mystery of "sculpting in time" is not a simple concept, but it explains my first principle of dramaturgy: *form*. The second principle, *action*, is even more apt to be underestimated, probably because *action* is so common a word in English that it hides rather than reveals its full Aristotelian sense as a term of art. Action is not "a story," it is not strenuous agitation (sword fights onstage, for instance). It is, in its deeper sense an inner essence of being alive, and it operates in every living moment until we die. Then it stops. *Action* is thus inescapable except that it inevitably will end. That catastrophe is inescapable. The theatre was invented to display this mystery, and to do so "live." I have frequently wished we had a better word for it in English, and that is why I often substitute Aristotle's *praxis*, as a way of signaling that the meaning is harder than you think. The term has nothing to do with Realism: abstract art is *an action*. Studied as a principle, *action* and its deep fusion with *time*, puts all theatre artists, musicians, dancers, and filmmakers on the right artistic path to be *poets* in its ancient meaning: makers, fabricators of art "objects." Those entities are only metaphorically called "objects" in the case of the *time-arts* of performance.

My argument and my teaching are based on elemental underlying truths about playmaking (which is itself an *action*) and the medium of the drama (which is structured time). I use playmaking to include several disciplines usually differentiated from each other – especially in relation to dramaturgy. The term "playmaking" is chosen to include playwriting, directing (especially the important work of what have come to be known as "*auteur–directors,*" an interesting and telltale neologism), acting, stage management, and design in all its aspects: sets, costumes, lighting, props, and sound – all of them incongruously bundled into a single catch-all phrase. Each discipline is habitually separated from the larger collective task of "composing for the stage" – especially during training in schools and universities. But our terms reveal a *subordination* of disciplines, whose practitioners are marshaled like troops under the central authority usually of a director. Dramaturgy addresses the unifying goal all these specializations are supposed to share: the making of *one thing* – usually called "a play," but as often in contemporary practice called a "performance piece." Dramaturgy might well be defined as the unified field theory of playmaking in all its aspects, whether *representational* or *presentational*.

What I envision here for theatre art is analogous to what T.S. Eliot envisioned for poetry when he wrote, "real poetry survives not only a change of popular opinion but the complete extinction of interest in the issues with which the poet was passionately concerned" (Eliot, 1957, p. 17). The study of dramaturgy is not an end in itself, it is a means to full activation of capacity as a creative artist. "The aim of technique is to free the spirit," said Martha Graham, speaking of dance; it is true of playmaking too. All technique is founded on arduously discovered principles.

The two principles

Principles of Dramaturgy has been boiled down to two inescapable dramatic principles: *action* and *form*. It is my contention, as it was Aristotle's, that action and form are the invariant bedrock of all dramatic art – and I would add something Aristotle had no reason to consider: that this is so regardless of style, historical period, subject matter, or culture. Action and form are presented as *principles*, and on these two principles, thoroughly understood, swift progress can be made toward the fully competent, flexible, and infinitely creative practice of theatrical art. Furthermore, in addressing what most frequently goes wrong in theatre practice, at whatever level of professionalism, I have found no serious error which cannot be traced to either one or the other of these principles: either a fogginess about *action* (what the term means and what one is), or a neglect of *form* – and underestimation of the *artifactual* nature of a play, or of *any* performance piece. This book seeks to gain maximum leverage on *practice* with a foundational discourse on the fewest possible principles. It also suggests methods for implementing these principles while composing for the stage, or writing the script for a play.

The shibboleth of "Realism," and the postulation of the "postdramatic"

My book has little to do with "Realism," but it does use many examples from the historical stock of plays that makes up the conventional catalogue of dramatic literature. When readers discern that I am not hostile to Realism, which I consider only one distinguishing style among many in the long history of the theatre, they should refrain from reaching the wrong conclusion. I am not expressing a preference so much as I am deliberately avoiding controversies about contemporary practices and plays. My contention is that there are principles that apply to *all* theatrical styles. I chose deliberately to draw examples from the whole gamut of past dramatic literature, from the ancient Greeks to Samuel Beckett. Discussions of *action*, especially when it gets around to the actions of *characters* within fictional settings, will (I suspect) sound at first distressingly "conventional" to many contemporary students, and also (perhaps especially) to their current teachers. Students of the theatre are understandably eager for a style in step with these rapidly shifting times – and there is a good argument to be made that the twenty-first century has already left not only *postmodernism*, but even the *après-post* era behind. The term "postdramatic" suggests a complete break with any previous culture, practice, or assumptions. The term seems to cement in a satisfying way a long, deep, often semi-conscious prejudice against Realism – a prejudice that is especially prevalent (for some strange reason) in America. The term Realism is often used side-by-side with the phrase "conventional theatre," something that the defiant term "postdramatic" promises to break away from decisively. But nothing could be more alien and distorting than to impute such motives to the *avant-garde* artists Hans Thies Lehmann collected for his study of the "postdramatic" (Lehmann, 2006). Even the ShowBiz journal *par excellence*, *Variety*, reserves a taxonomic distinction for what it calls the "legit" theatre.

A difficulty arises if "postdramatic" has acquired the burden of meaning the polar opposite of "conventional." It then misleads by suggesting that the "game" of theatre is now under an obligation to be played without rules. Every artist is supposed to hate rules, and "principles" sounds like "rules." If one were building furniture (chairs and tables, for instance) a useful *principle* would be an appreciation of gravity, and its inevitable role in the craftsman's art. The concepts of "level" and "vertical" or "square" are direct expressions of the single inescapable *principle* of gravity, and very specific tools – carpenter's levels and carpenter's squares – are basic tools that *govern* carpentry. Architecture has an identical foundational relation to gravity, and with it to strength of materials and *principles* of load bearing, and stability of structures. No one can practice either carpentry or architecture without a close compliance with principles of this kind (in this case all founded on gravity). Even (or especially) a Frank Gehry, whose buildings *seem* to have broken loose entirely from the "constraint" of gravity, and thus from any "conventional" architecture, is still operating within an inescapable principle. In fact and in practice, Frank Gehry's buildings are monstrously obsessed with gravity, especially with the complicated construction that *respects* gravity (as it must) while giving the visual impression that gravity is irrelevant. Completely analogously, classical nineteenth-century ballet technique sought to give the *impression* that dancers were exempted from the "law" of gravity. So-called "modern" dance returned to a celebration of gravity, and a deep "organic" acknowledgment of its force on the human body. Is this a constraining conventional "rule," or is it an underlying principle? The balletic gravity-defying *convention* was an aesthetic, and it can still elicit wonder when practiced by a trained master. But it has also been rebelled against as brutally anti-naturalistic, inorganic, and hatefully abusive of dancer's bodies. A ballerina's tutu conceals and disguises a musculature necessary for lifts and soaring bird-flight leaps, just as a Frank Gehry building conceals a huge armature of supporting frames and *trompe-l'oeil* reinforcements carrying the inevitable structural loads of any huge inhabited building. Aesthetic fashions and accepted conventions differ from principles, which if formulated accurately *underlie* all fashions of taste and habits of practice.

I worked with many so-called "postdramatic" practitioners who were supported and encouraged by Ellen Stewart at Cafe La MaMa E.T.C., Joe Papp at the Public Theater, Saint Mark's Church-in-the-Bowery, and Bob Wilson's Byrd Hoffman School of Byrds – in short the off-off-Broadway theatre in New York City. But I had also been raised in France, and "forced" to attend from an early age the Comédie Française and the Théâtre National Populaire. We also were obliged, in French public school, to memorize and recite famous passages and tirades from Corneille and Molière, from Beaumarchais and Edmond Rostand, along with longish poems by La Fontaine and Villon, Lamartine and Victor Hugo. I shared these European continental experiences with such New York *avant-gardistes* as Jean-Claude van Itallie (who was raised speaking French in Belgium) and the founding members of Mabou Mines, who had met each other while ex-pats in Paris. All of us were formed under the influence of Samuel Beckett and Eugène Ionesco, Fernando Arrabal and Jean Genet (all of whom I eventually met). Add to these cohorts Joe Chaikin, Richard

Foreman, the young Sam Shepard... these were the American theatre artists who anchored my career and my own aesthetic. We were all strenuously differentiating ourselves not from "the dramatic," but from the demoralizing commercialized Broadway ShowBiz. If anything, we thought of ourselves as rescuing the drama from the commodified (and debased) stage trade in big-money profit-seeking blockbusters. These young turks and their theatre practice *clarified* the principles I enunciate in this book. Nothing was more refreshing and inspiring, or more fundamentally *dramatic*, as I would use the term, than say Lee Breuer's *Shaggy Dog Animation*, or Richard Foreman's *Pandering to the Masses*. In addition, I trained deeply in the long history of the theatre, and the canonical classics: Aeschylus, Sophocles, Euripides, Plautus, Terence, medieval Mysteries, the *Commedia dell'arte*, Shakespeare, Tirso de Molina, Racine, Molière, Goldoni, Beaumarchais, Goethe, Schiller, Victor Hugo, Ibsen, Strindberg.... I am not hostile to the historical tradition, even the late-nineteenth century's "bourgeois" *boulevard* sex farces, against which the Modernist *avant-gardistes* rebelled so strenuously a century and a half ago. Jarry's *Ubu Roi* is as welcome in my repertoire as is Feydeau's *Occupe-toi d'Amélie*; Aristophanes' *Thesmophoriazusae* observes the same principles as does Wilson's *Einstein on the Beach*.

In what follows, I stay by and large away from any discussion of specific contemporary American playwrights. The exception is Robert Wilson, and I use *Einstein on the Beach* (which incidentally exerted a huge personal influence on me) mainly to show that Bob's work illustrates as well as Arthur Miller's or Lope de Vega's would have, principles that have nothing to do with Realism.

Presentational and representational theatres

The distinction between "dramatic" and "postdramatic" which Professor Hans Thies Lehmann introduced into current discourse is really a distinction between representational and presentational uses of a theatre. Let me align such terms with the ensuing principles in this book. *All* theatre is presentational. *That* reality is the in-your-face reality of live performance. Some (historically, perhaps *most*) theatre has been and continues to be also representational. The relevant distinction has to do with adding a fictional layer to performance. An analogy to "abstract" and "realistic" painting might be helpful.

All painting is artifice. The *subject* in painting, and its treatment on the canvas, are what differentiate Realism from abstract painting. But both remain the application of a pigment ooze to a surface. The most meticulously photographic (or *trompe-l'oeil*) Realism in painting is still completely artifactual. Similarly, "abstract" painting invariably still has a subject. It simply shifts from a *represented subject* somewhere outside the painting to the *presented* world of the painting itself. The great twentieth-century painter Camille Souter (who is still painting strongly at ninety), has often been characterized – especially in her early work – as an "abstract" painter, but she has always contested the term. She once told me explicitly, "If it hasn't subject matter, it simply doesn't work." She added, "I would call my paintings more symbols than abstracts." There have been periods in artistic fashion when a surface verisimilitude has been very highly prized. That fashion and that taste are no longer dominant in the art world (yet they persist in innumerable individual art lovers), but they tended to coincide with the heyday of Realism in the theatre, an era now more than a century behind us. Starting with the late-nineteenth-century French Impressionists, a process of "abstraction" set in dramatically in the world of painting. The Picasso revolution that followed pushed the European world into cubism (where the "subject" was still distinctly legible) and beyond into "full abstraction" in the works of such artists as Willem de Kooning, Jackson Pollock, and Mark Rothko. One might say that the "subject" became the painting itself, and the "action" was the action of the painter while making the painting. It is no mere coincidence that the critic Clement Greenberg coined the term "action painting" for these New York artists. So-called "abstract" paintings are a pure and open record of the visual–poetics of composition and painting. The canvas *becomes* the subject. These well-named "action painters" serve as our best analogies to the theatrical *avant-garde* and the increasingly *presentational* uses of performance spaces. For artists like Robert Wilson, Richard Foreman, Liz LeCompte, Lee Breuer, or Anne Bogart, the performance "canvas" *is* the subject. The action of the piece is *their* action, of composition and presentation. There is no supervening or displacing fiction involved.

This game of *fiction*, when it is played in the "conventional" theatre, is what calls for the famous suspension of disbelief, for going along with an illusion. But at its core, the theatre is never any other reality than itself. The fully presentational mode of theatre is not new, but ancient. It is the natural mode for this art form. Yet just because we have rediscovered a theatrical equivalent to abstract art, it would be foolish to discount theatre's compelling capacity to impose *the illusion of the real*. As a cultural instrument, the theatre has allowed human beings to indulge in a safe "double-take" on lived experience. In tragedy, for instance, theatrical practice has allowed audiences to learn from (by witnessing) catastrophic experience that scapegoat–protagonists do not survive. But the actors survive. We have learned to take that "double-take" for granted.

Sacrificial victims have all-too literally played the scapegoat role since prehistoric times, when ritual killing fascinated those (like ourselves) who realized they were mortal, who were always frightened, under constant threat. The advent of "conventionalized" cultural locations in which to see such ritual enactments and re-enactments gave rise to elaborate sacred "seeing-places" which still survive from antiquity. The move from human victim to scapegoat, and again from a goat to a representation, *is* the history of the theatre. In what follows, I have sought to describe what has never changed in that *theatron*. There are principles by which the three plays of the *Oresteia* and Lee Breuer's *Red Horse Animation* are firmly linked. The *plot* of Agamemnon's homecoming from Troy is as necessary and unavoidable as is the *plot* of Hamm's endgame. It is not a superficial resemblance that links the two plays to identical principles. Both works use the same canvas: a time-form that reveals itself in performance. Those bedrock connections are craft principles, and they can be used wrong, or ineptly. It is useful to learn them, and learn how to apply them. In this book they are addressed as dramaturgy. They apply identically to representational and presentational theatre modalities, for whenever you structure time, you perform an action. When I mention Aristotle (as I will frequently) I advise the reader *not* to jump to the conclusion that I mean "Realism" or "conventional dramaturgy." Aristotle's formal insights have been often misjudged, and his name has in many periods enraged those who feel compelled to question authority and break constraining "rules." I endorse such rebellion, and I assure you at the outset there is no contradiction in teaching unapologetically from Aristotle.

References

Eliot, T.S. (1957) "The Social Function of Poetry" in *On Poetry and Poets*. London: Faber and Faber.

Lehmann, H.T. (2006) *Post Dramatic Theatre*. Translated from German by K. Jürs-Munby. New York: Routledge. (Originally published 1999.)

Acknowledgments

This book would not exist without the timely and devoted assistance of Magda Romanska and Owen Doyle, who took charge of editing the original manuscript and finalizing the text. Owen also oversaw the preparation of the illustrations. He did this because he believed in the book, the contents of which he has been acquainted with for many years, as an undergraduate student at M.I.T., as a graduate dramaturgy student at Harvard, and as a serious actor and playwright. A prior and crucial supporter of this book was John Gregory Kulka, now at the Library of America, without whom this manuscript would not have found its way to Magda, and thus to Routledge.

The book grew out of my many years as Literary Director of Robert Brustein's and Robert Orchard's American Repertory Theatre (A.R.T.), in particular my role as Director of the Dramaturgy and Playwriting Programs at the Institute for Advanced Theatre Training at Harvard, an offshoot of the A.R.T. Bob and Rob (as Brustein and Orchard were referred to by all who worked for them) are to be thanked and commended for creating these institutions and for plunging me into the field of dramaturgy. It is because they entrusted me with devising and teaching a comprehensive curriculum for the training of professional dramaturgs that this book was written. The Swiss theatre director, François Rochaix, while Director of the A.R.T. Institute, assisted me in extending this training to all our graduate students in acting and directing.

Undergraduates at Harvard College were also offered these subjects through the Dramatic Arts Curriculum, overseen at the College by the Committee on Dramatics and its two faculty chairs during my time at A.R.T., Dean Michael Shinagel and Professor Robert Kiely who each deserve their share of thanks. The many students, graduate and undergraduate, who studied dramaturgy with me are too numerous to thank individually here, but I think particularly of David Gammons, Gideon Lester, Kate Whoriskey, Chris Baker, Dorothee Hannapel, Jennie Knapp, Jill

Robbins, Sarah Stevenson, Carol Verburg, Chris Tiffany, Monika Gay, Amanda Gann, Shawn René Graham, Heather Helinsky, Aoife Spillane-Hinks, and Jason Fitzgerald, the last of whom went further than anyone in urging publication, and who shared the book in manuscript with his students at Columbia as well as among his many colleagues in Performance Studies.

A special group of brave and determined souls elected to make theatre practice their "major," despite the fact that there was no official department or degree in this field when they were undergraduates. Their concentrated study with me refined every aspect of this book, which was developed as the core of their curriculum. I acknowledge here Meg Kerr, Elizabeth Mak, Christine Bendorf, James Leaf, Calla Videt, Sophie Kargman, Michael Donohue, Scottie Thompson, Maria Gambale, and Todd Kessler.

The late Roger Shattuck at Boston University read an early draft and endorsed the book as it was then conceived. Harvard Professor emeritus Jurij Striedter read my chapter on action and gave erudite notes on the bewildering array of ways Aristotle's *praxis* has been translated and understood in many languages throughout history. Professor Jeffrey Hause at Creighton University double-checked all I wrote about Aristotle, Aquinas, and Saint Augustine, and adjusted for accuracy in several places. Professor Ángel Berenguer gave me many opportunities to present dramaturgical ideas and techniques at the University of Alcalá and at the University of Granada. Our mutual student, now Professor Diego Santos Sánchez at the Complutense University in Madrid, translated my "diagramas de cuentas" and my words about them into Spanish for talks I gave at the Ateneo de Madrid. And Sir Christopher Ricks supported my work by giving me recurring opportunities to speak on my subject at his Editorial Institute at Boston University and at the annual conference of the Association of Literary Scholars, Critics, and Writers (A.L.S.C.W.). James Bundy and Catherine Sheehy invited me to Yale to speak about dramaturgy at the School of Drama.

The stage directors Robert Wilson, Anne Bogart, Joe Dowling, François Rochaix, and Andrei Belgrader were, among all the directors with whom I have worked as dramaturg, the most generous, inspiring, and appreciative of the principles as I formulated them. Many faculty colleagues in the English Department at Harvard encouraged the book unceasingly: Elaine Scarry, Phil Fisher, James Engell, Stephen Greenblatt, Daniel Albright, Marc Shell, James Simpson, Nicholas Watson, Daniel Donoghue, Peter Sacks, Helen Vendler, Joseph Harris, Gordon Teskey, Werner Sollors, and John Stauffer. Beyond these, this book owes a great debt of gratitude to the regular stimulation provided by members of Professor Emeritus

Donald Fanger's eponymous "Fanger Table," Dean Henry Rosovsky, Gretchen and Barry Mazur, Pat and Loren Graham, the late and much beloved Daniel Aaron, Bill Todd, and of course, Fanger himself. One could not wish for more valued literary and scholarly friends.

For refuge and tranquility, this writing project is immeasurably indebted to Alfie and Sally Alcorn, who lent me the use of their cabin in the Berkshires, as well as to Bart and Doris Noyes who facilitated the same in New Hampshire. John F. Deane arranged access for me to the Heinrich Böll cottage on Achill Island, County Mayo, where the manuscript was finished.

And of course, there are my wife and son, to whom the book is dedicated – *intelligenti pauca*.

Introduction
What is dramaturgy?

Dramaturgy is a generalized craft–knowledge needed by *everyone* who works in the theatre. Everyone involved in theatre practices dramaturgy, whether they credit themselves consciously with this skill or not. Every properties assistant backstage, every lighting operator running cues, every stage hand shifting sets, and every usher in the house has a distinct perception of whether a scene in progress, on any given night, is going well or badly. That knowledge is practical dramaturgy at work. Actors monitor themselves throughout each performance, and the best ones adjust constantly to shifting dramaturgical conditions. Directors, long after their contracts expire (usually on opening night) continue to imagine and participate in their productions. Playwrights agonize endlessly over plays they have composed, second-guessing scenes and passages, lines and responses long after they have been passed through the rigors of rehearsal and the trials of public performance. And the public – the least predictable agent in theatre-making – practices dramaturgy with the least training and with devastating finality. Their response to a play determines the ultimate success or failure of the whole expensive and time-consuming enterprise of playmaking. Dramaturgy is everybody's business.

But it is also the specific business of a particular employee in many theatres: the resident dramaturg. For this person, dramaturgy is a specialization and a profession, and it requires a precise definition linked to performable duties. The dramaturg holds the one position in the theatre that most frequently provokes the question, "Now what is it that you do, exactly…?" No one seems quite able to understand or to retain the gist of a description of what a dramaturg is, or what one does. The reason for this is that no single, clear definition of a dramaturg exists.

In America, in the nineteenth century, theatres used to call in a guy with a knack who could help save a situation that was heading toward disaster. This practical handyman was known colloquially as the "script doctor," and that was clearly an early form of the dramaturg. But the function varies with the project, and a dramaturg on a production of a new play will have a completely different role from that of a dramaturg on the production of an established classic. The term dramaturg itself (which many find an awkward, ugly word in English) is imported from (and still sounds) German. The granddaddy of all dramaturgs, everyone seems to agree, was Gotthold Ephraim Lessing (1729–1781), whose 1769 book of essays, *Hamburgische Dramaturgie* (Lessing, 1962), both introduced the term and established the role of a well-educated, critically-minded literary type who would busy himself in the practical production of plays, rather than simply ranting and railing about them from his study.

From a historical perspective, then, dramaturgy might be described as a discipline invented by critics in retroactive dismay over what they had seen on the stage. Defined thus dramaturgy assigns itself the uncomfortable mission of upbraiding current practitioners of the drama (the least pleasant aspect of criticism) while simultaneously attempting to upgrade the intellectual tone and the *quality* of what is presented in the theatre.

In Greek, *dramatourgos* has exactly the same etymological roots as the word *playwright* in English: it means one who works in the material of the drama, i.e., who *makes* plays; the term is analogous to *shipwright*, or *wheelwright*, in that it focuses attention on craft and construction. To this day, the word *dramaturge* means *playwright* in France, for instance, and it is a professional label good enough for a French "carte d'identité." By extension, *dramaturgy* focuses the mind on craft questions encountered while fashioning viable plays for the stage. A parallel term in English is *metallurgy*, which denotes the craft of working in metals. Such nuts-and-bolts usage is the sense aimed at in this book. The presence in a machine shop of a *metallurgist* does not imply that the machinists are all incompetent, and in need of correction. But a metallurgist will know things even a seasoned machinist can never learn from practice alone. In an ideal world, no working dramaturg would be burdened with the implication that she is in the theatre *because* her fellow workers cannot be trusted to get things right on their own. The remedial model of the role of the dramaturg, while accurate historically, is inadequate in the contemporary theatre, where "artistic collaborator" is a better model and description of the role intended for dramaturgs. The goal of contemporary dramaturgy can be stated more simply as that of enriching the theatre with breadth of knowledge, insight, and accuracy of information.

With the understanding that the specific duties of professional dramaturgs will be described in detail, it will be helpful in following this book overall to think of dramaturgy as a *function*, and not uniquely as a specialization. Dramaturgy is a function that must be exercised by everyone actively at work on play production, starting with the director (who should ideally be the best versed in dramaturgy), and extending to the designers, the actors, stage management, the producer, and all other personnel with any connection to the production. Dramaturgy requires real skills, and everyone who works inside the theatre should constantly be deepening and refining their knowledge of what plays are and how they work.

The basic principles

Form: time and the plot-bead diagram

The book begins with form, which is the central mystery of the art of the drama. In all performance arts, *time* is the difficult medium. Lessing wrote an extended aesthetic essay, *Laocoön*, a year before he embarked on *Hamburg Dramaturgy* (i.e., in 1766). In this powerful critical study, Lessing usefully differentiated *performing* arts (shaped in time) from the *plastic* arts (shaped in space). Spatial form might be *analogous* to temporal form but the two media of space and time have distinct and immiscible properties. In one case, the relations between parts are rhythmic (i.e., governed by pace, tempo, and duration) whereas in the other case, the relations between parts are spatial (i.e., governed by shape, location, and intervening space). In painting, sculpture and architecture we examine (or determine, if we are composing in the medium) *where* the "parts" of the composition are in relation to each other. In music, dance, and theatre we examine (or determine, if we are composing in the medium) *when* the parts occur in relation to each other, and how long each "part" lasts, and at what tempo. The plastic artwork is bounded in space, the time-form of a performance piece is bounded by its beginning and its end in time.

A "plot-bead diagram" is a visual representation of time and is possible for *any* performance event, whatever its style of representation may be, whatever its subject matter (see examples in Figure I.1). Music can be plot-beaded, and in fact a musical score *is* a detailed, note-by-note plot-bead diagram. The plot-bead diagram and its uses will be introduced in Chapter 1, but suffice it to say here that it is a working tool that makes visually obvious that dramatic performance must necessarily begin at some determinable point in time, and that it must inevitably proceed and come to an end at some equally specific and recognizable closing moment. The plot-bead diagram represents the play as a series of "event beads" strung end to end on a thread – the "thread" being in essence a time-line. The succeeding beads on the time-line represent *units of duration*, and the key insight (a legacy of Aristotle) is that these succeeding "events" are the formal units of composition in the artifact we call a play. The plot-bead diagram is drawn such that the beads appear in the drawing in the same

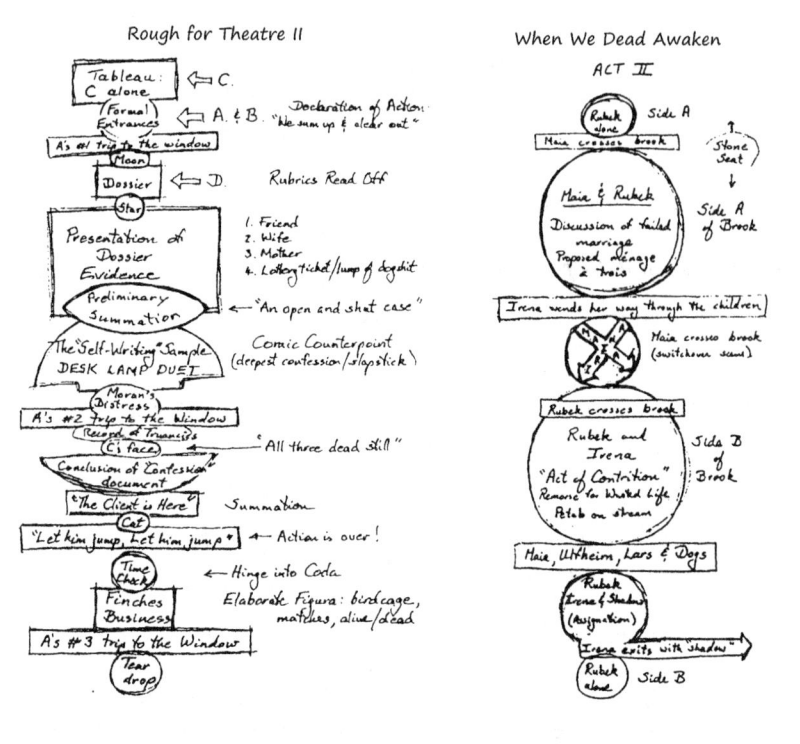

Figure I.1 Example plot-bead diagrams – Samuel Beckett's *Rough for Theatre II* and Henrik Ibsen's *When We Dead Awaken*, Act II.

sequence as the events they represent; they chart the course of the performance through time. The result is a formal map of the play, drawn such that the mind can grasp it as "one thing," a formal whole. This "grasp" is another word for formal mastery.

Paradoxically, it is easier to discern pure theatrical *form* in frankly anti-realist, stylized work (like that of the mis-labeled "postdramatic" practitioners discussed in the preface: Mabou Mines, Richard Foreman, The Wooster Group, or Robert Wilson) than in conventional theatre. It is paradoxical because the "lifelike" or realistic theatrical convention *masks* formal construction whereas abstract work *reveals* it: the theatrical artifact is more visible when the "story" is absent or de-emphasized. American audiences are most baffled on those occasions of greatest artistic clarity, and this explains the rift that occurs between popular taste and an esoteric craving, among artists, for the "pure" experience of formal construction and experimentation. We can gauge how deep-seated the popular American appetite for "life-likeness" is when we notice that it is formal transparency that baffles the comprehension of the average theatregoer. Thus, in studying *form* we need to balance the popular predilection for Realism against the artist/craftsman's need to see past representation to shaped and manipulated form. There are deep artisanal reasons for insisting on a clear intellection of form alone, before returning (since we must) to all the distracting details of such "old-fashioned" elements as subject, story, characters, setting, historical periods, colloquial diction, and other popular habits of stylization. Form underlies all variations in style, and Chapter 1 will explain how the plot-bead diagram can be used to study and manipulate the time-form of a play (as well as increase awareness of it) regardless of the style of the play.

A further confusion on the topic of dramatic form (the *plot-form* created in time) derives from the fact that there has been a visual revolution in the theatre in the twentieth century. The theatre has always been spectacle, but in the past century, the visual treatment of the stage has achieved both theoretical prominence and dizzying technological development. If we compare the "standard" painted drops and wings of the end of the nineteenth century to the fully architectural treatment of productions today (I speak of those that are well-funded, naturally) and their full bath of complexly controlled light, we can see that the visual elements tend to compete with the traditional plot (and the story it so often tells) for the audience's primary attention. Some people love this, others hate it. My dramaturgy students at the American Repertory Theatre one year developed a glib but telling shorthand for the aesthetic of Robert Brustein's theatre: "*Opsis* at the expense of *Praxis*," or *spectacle* at the expense of *action*. This was unfair, but they had just been immersed in the study of Aristotle's *Poetics*, and they reflected a good understanding of two terms Aristotle ranked at opposite ends of his hierarchy of elements of the drama, with spectacle ranked least important. Most reviewers expect some common-sense balance between spectacle and intrinsic dramatic interest, with the more conventional critics (i.e., the ones who most reflect public taste) favoring the idea that *setting* should be at the service of a plot structure that adds up to something in its own right – not the other way around. The A.R.T., in the 20 years after its founding, when Robert Brustein was its artistic leader, frequently put off its patrons by letting set and scenic effect overwhelm more traditional expectations in the theatre. Without taking sides in this aesthetic debate, dramaturgy remains centered in the temporal *plot*, and thus at some remove from purely spatial and visual stagecraft. But Robert Wilson, again, is the artist who crosses the line between the two styles: in his theatre, the visual and architectural "book" becomes the chief structure of the *plot*, and the whole organization of the spectacle is conceived abstractly as a time-form, very much as though it were a fully-realized architectural/visual "music." His example has transformed the theatre in Europe, and it helps clarify the formal terms I introduce here, because it makes clear their essential independence from Realism. In the realistic, representational style, the formal plot elements are just as *present* and just as contrived as they are in a Wilson composition, but they are harder to discern in the blurred perceptual slurry of "life-likeness," which is an audience's point of view, not a theatre–artist's. Finally, form is neglected for a deeply intuitive reason that is rarely discussed. *Form* is misleadingly associated with suspected *constraints* on an idealized (and erroneous) notion of artistic freedom.

Action: human "doings" and knowing what we're doing

Chapter 2 takes up the concept of *action*, which in its technical sense is the description of a human "doing." The theatre invariably deals in human "doings" (not just in the *results* of deeds and events, which are over and done with). The stress in the drama is firmly on the active present-tense spectacle of human beings in the act of "doing." That is what *performance* means, and the drama – whatever its style – is a performance art. We depart from the essence of theatre when we leave the immediate vicinity of a "deed-in-progress," and this is why the central art in the theatre is "acting" – invariably and accurately described with a present participle, a verb form that is engaged in the present. "Performance" is already a cooler term than "acting," for it is already more abstract, less focused in time, vaguely generic, already detached from the immediacy of human witness and human action in present time. But *performance* better describes non-representational actions, the purely presentational mode that is freed from a fictional obligation. The ancient Greek word "drama" was derived (Aristotle tells us) from the Attic verb of doing ($\delta\rho\alpha\nu$ = "to do") and no theatrical style of performance in any period of history has ever altered the fundamental situation that defines "theatre": a real-time "doing" witnessed by an audience of assembled spectators. Thus, both theoretically and practically, all drama (and dramaturgy) begins and ends in *action*.

Obvious as this action-center may seem in defining the theatre, action awareness is the most haphazard and uneven of qualities to be found in the profession. *Action* is not obvious to everyone, and *dramaturgical* savvy consists in spotting action-problems swiftly and knowing what to do about a perceived gap or flaw in the action of a patch of text trying to activate itself into drama.

The paramount importance of *action* is compounded further for those artists in the room who happen to be actors, for in their case they are doing what *they* are supposed to be doing when their bodies and minds are focused specifically on *action*. Actors are on top of their game when they know (in the representational mode) what their *characters* are supposed to be doing. Thus, it is not unreasonable to expect an actor to know exactly how to seek and find an action, or how to answer the elementary question, "What is my character doing?" And unlike the bland colloquial sense in which it would be nice in *all* professional situations if people "knew what they were doing," for actors, "knowing what you're *doing*" is clearly a term of art.

We still owe most of our action awareness in the theatre to Stanislavski. No one more assiduously analyzed, formulated, promulgated, and evangelized the Holy Grail of action than he did. But if Stanislavski and his disciples can be credited, at least in the United States, with giving wide currency to *action* in the training of actors, this discipline has not, for various reasons, equally illuminated the rest of the field. Certainly would-be playwrights are seldom given any clue to the nature and constitutive importance of action – unless, of course, they come from acting backgrounds rather than writing or literature backgrounds. But in the case of actors-turned-playwrights, what they know of *action* they have either deduced empirically or learned from some exposure to one of the Stanislavski-based schools of acting training. Other theatre artists – designers, producers, dramaturgs, and, most distressingly, directors (even when they come from a background in acting) – consistently underestimate the structural and formal importance of *action* and thus fail to grasp its centrality to the art of the drama. They may pay it lip service but otherwise ignore its full range of implications and the consequences of its meaning in creating a performance.

Worse yet, academic literary studies since the late 1960s have, in their ever-narrowing concentration on textuality and the evanescent quandaries of *linguistic* representations of consciousness, missed the boat completely on action as an *underlying* compositional principle. The urge to deconstruct has not proven to be very productive in the theatre, but nothing could more empower that urge toward innovative playmaking than an understanding of the *action* involved in the critical process itself. Neither Jacques Derrida nor Paul de Man could have written a word of deconstructive criticism had they not been in the grip of an *action* that was in progress in their minds and imaginations. That action can be imagined, and once imagined, it can be imitated and it can shape a play. In a conventional play, the shaping action is the action of a fictional character, or of a cluster of characters all drawn into the sphere of a central *represented* action (the action of the play). In a non-conventional performance piece, the shaping action is usually that of the composing artist, who is "acting out" an attitude (or sometimes a theory) toward art, toward society, or toward his or her imagined audience. This self-conscious action is also, in such works, "the action of the play."

Applying the principals

With the twin principles of form and action thoroughly discussed, we shift our focus to modes of application of these principles. Chapter 3 introduces the specific job of *Production Dramaturgy*, which must be differentiated from the more general functions of a Literary Manager. As a rough rule, Literary Manager is a "front office" job, and production dramaturg (it may well be performed by the same person) implies direct engagement in the rehearsal hall.

The Literary Manager typically has the following four areas of responsibility:

1   season planning, which requires a vast knowledge of dramatic literature matched to an informed sensitivity to audience demand and/or the careers of individual actors in a repertory company;
2   reading and evaluating scripts, old and new, which entails a great deal of reading time, reflection, analytical acumen and seasoned judgment;
3   public "enrichment" via writing and speaking, or the publication of newsletters, program notes, study guides, and the organization and presentation of symposia, Q&A sessions, and other corollary cultural offerings (distinct from publicity); and
4   archiving and documentation: the orderly preservation of theatre history generated by the theatre.

Production Dramaturgy (the subject of Chapter 3) is practiced in three principal modes:

1   Standard Production Dramaturgy, which accompanies the production of a finished, pre-existing play, whether a classic or a lesser play from the dramatic repertoire.
2   New Play Development, which shepherds and assists the premier presentation of a new script; remedial ghost playwriting is always involved, but problematically so.
3   Translation and/or Adaptation, which partakes of the dramaturgy of both, for a translation is both "pre-existing" and new. The development and field-testing of new translations from the international repertoire should be a constant original contribution of professional dramaturgs to theatre culture.

Chapter 3 introduces a full methodology for the practice of Production Dramaturgy, from the selection of plays for production, through planning stages and "enrichment" periods characterized by analysis and research. Chapter 3 was developed over several years when I was Director of the Dramaturgy Program at the Institute for Advanced Theatre Training at Harvard. It is the blueprint for a two-year graduate MFA program in Dramaturgy. The chapter discusses the complex decision-making that determines "the take this time"– or how a play will be handled in a *particular* production – and finally details what dramaturgs do during rehearsals, tracking the process all the way to its culmination in performance.

Structural conflicts of Production Dramaturgy

It is always a delicate matter to discuss openly a certain anti-analytical prejudice that pervades the American theatre (more so, for instance, than the European theatre). There seems to be a deep-seated notion that critical or analytical thinking threatens and destroys the infinite prerogatives of creative genius. This notion seems to be based on what I have come to call the replacement theory of genius: the conviction that whatever portion of the creative psyche is colonized by training in technique is stolen from the realm of pure creativity.

No one in the theatre is more directly in the path of this prejudice than is the production dramaturg – whose job it is, in large part, to be analytical. The typical operation of the prejudice characterizes (and dismisses) a dramaturg's input as mere learned *opinion* about the play, something devoid of passion and useless for actors.

The idea that "thoughts" cannot appeal to the emotions is a prejudice. A well-trained dramaturg's opinions about a play *should* differ in kind and quality from run-of-the-mill opinions, and the disciplined and patient ruminations of a good dramaturg should be considered on a different plane from an actor's or a director's first impressions of a script. Put even more bluntly, vivid first impressions have all-too frequently been the sole determinant of production decisions and values, whereas the model of play production that makes room for a production dramaturg opens a door to second thoughts about first impressions. There is a notoriously volatile quality to first impressions, which are characteristically narrow, impulsive, and yet long-lasting. A greater lateral reach into context and nuance generally mellows the first impression, and for many who deal in the highly charged world of theatricality, that mellowing is instinctively an undesirable thing – something to be resisted. Thus, the dramaturg, trained to have second thoughts about first impressions, seems to dissipate rather than enhance the impulsive energy of strong first impressions. Many high-strung directors instinctively intuit that whatever may be gained by context and insight is equally likely to blunt the impact and immediacy of first contact with an unfamiliar thing. This clash between impulse and reflection is the very essence of dramaturgical interaction, and both poles should influence the other. Since an audience will have (usually) *only* a first encounter with the finished production, those who are orchestrating that production will want the event to have originality, punch, and impact. By comparison, depth, nuance, and breadth of reference can seem secondary values. Show business is essentially defined by this tug-of-war between competing standards of excellence – on the one hand, immediate pizzazz, energy, and knock-your-socks-off theatricality, and on the other, cultural and historical richness, thoughtfulness, depth of information, insight, and intellectual "seriousness." The showbiz side of the profession fears and mistrusts the "high art" side of the dramaturgical divide, while the cultural and intellectual faction that claims a stake in the theatre deplores the cheap tricks and vulgar methods of "immediacy" in the theatre, whether these are achieved via spectacle or via the cultivation of novelty – which favors the *feel* of first impressions.

Ideally, the best directors and actors should also be expected to be expert dramaturgs, in its extended sense, and there are methods by which to increase the authority and validity of *anyone's* dramaturgical opinions, and thus place them above others in value. This is a crucial point, and the relative *value* of various opinions (i.e., informed and uninformed ones) should not be ascribed as though they were intrinsic to assigned roles in a production team. Actors and directors should be just as eager as the production dramaturg to have "expert" opinions about a script. Stanislavski – to his credit – also acknowledged this point, for he made the following remark about preparatory work on a script:

> Let the reader learn from experienced literary people how to pick out at once the heart of a work, the fundamental line of the emotions. A person trained in literature, who has studied the basic qualities of literary works, can instantly grasp the structure of a play, its points of departure, the feelings and thoughts which impelled the playwright to put pen to paper. This capacity is very helpful to an actor, so long as it does not interfere with his seeing for himself into the soul of the play.
>
> (Stanislavski, 1961, p. 6)

This is a good description of what is expected of a good production dramaturg. Once assigned to the production, he or she should be assumed to have a privileged "place at the table." Ideally this means that his or her take on the play might be expected (like the director's) to be a shaping influence on the production.

Production Dramaturgy is *participation* in creative work, not critical *judgment* of that work. This important distinction needs to be understood in the light of the fact that all intense creative work *includes* the constant application of critical judgment, but there is a crucial difference between engaged, dynamic, creative judgment and detached, static, and inhibiting criticism; the one shares responsibility for the outcome, the other stands aloof from it. No production dramaturg should practice without having learned in the rehearsal hall how to suppress the *negative* critical mode in favor of the *creative* one. Furthermore, the inherent *structural conflicts* between dramaturgs and directors often mar the practice of Production Dramaturgy. No director and no production dramaturg is fully trained and ready to practice without a thorough grounding in these areas of inadvertent (and frequently unsuspected) overlap. The director is granted, by convention and mutual understanding, a final and absolute artistic authority over a production.[1] But the dramaturg starts eroding that absolute authority the moment they start independently reading and analyzing the script, and ferreting about in outside source materials. Both analysis and research accumulate knowledge that carries an inevitable authority of its own. I call the resulting conflicts "structural" because they are generated not by personal animosity (though they can lead to or be exacerbated by personal animosity) but by a structural "authority overlap" that is inevitable. Dramaturgs will step on the absolute authority of a director by virtue of *knowing* something, and although anybody in a production might know any particular thing, it is the dramaturg's *job* to know it.

Directors and dramaturgs of good will can learn to recognize their overlapping *kinds* of authority and accept them with grace, but directors or dramaturgs who try to establish an absolute and autonomous authority within a production will clash inevitably as they perform their respective roles. The best remedy for such potential conflict is to secure the full consent of both parties to the "dramaturgical contract," as it might be called, before they begin their work; furthermore it is a good idea, where possible, to train both parties in techniques of collaboration. This has been the thrust of the training program in Dramaturgy at the Institute for Advanced Theatre Training at Harvard (which I headed from 1989 to 1997), where directors and dramaturgs studied dramaturgy together, in joint seminars. Directors who started working in the theatre before the dramaturg was added to the normal production process may resist this collaboration, but by now, the participation of an active production dramaturg is pretty well established in the non-commercial American theatre. Good contemporary directors, once sure of the basis of their own legitimate authority, offer little resistance to the full expression of the dramaturg's informational and analytical "authority."

The production dramaturg is frequently referred to as the dramatist's advocate, or the playwright's in-house spokesperson, and the reason for this collusive (and wryly adversarial) moniker is that disciplined analysis of the formal structures of a script *does* unearth powerful evidence of the author's intention. This raises the vexed question of a playscript's optimum interpretation as a score for performance, and of the playwright's *right* to have his or her play optimally produced, according to an original artistic design (or the audience's right to see that design if they pay to attend an event billed as that author's work). Dramaturgical analysis (shored up with a careful plot-bead diagram) quietly builds solid evidence for a focused – and to that extent delimiting – understanding of a play. Directors typically want complete control over the "take" or "reading" of the play they are about to direct. They are right in wanting to do so, for that take-charge willfulness demonstrates that they understand their aesthetic assignment and accept its large responsibility. Without prior experience of the processes of analysis, however, or an understanding of the epistemological status of the *results* of a dramaturg's systematic analysis, a director will feel pre-empted and hedged-in by any process that seems to produce answers to questions of interpretation that they (the director) would prefer to see remain open, especially during early stages of production. In insisting on this openness, however, directors can overplay their hand and close themselves off from extremely powerful understandings of the deep formal power already perfected for them by the (usually absent) playwright. The dramaturg has a responsibility to unearth this formal power, if it exists, and make it *available* for informed decisions about its use in each production. There may be some wrangling over legal, ethical, or aesthetic obligations to *use* the formal strengths of a script, but there is no defensible rationale for overlooking them.

Note

1   Subject to the even more final authority of the producer – an authority with the clout of market forces and contract law behind it, and therefore an authority beyond artistic considerations. Clashes between directors and producers are a different class of conflict altogether, and although they create a continuous tension within theatre culture (and remain perhaps the major unaddressed issue in American theatre practice) they typically have nothing to do with anything that properly comes under the rubric of dramaturgy.

References

Lessing, G.E. (1962) *Hamburg Dramaturgy*. Translated by H. Zimmern. New York: Dover Publications. (Originally published 1769.)

Stanislavski, K. (1961) *Creating a Role*. Translated by E.R. Hapgood. New York: Routledge. (Originally published 1936.)

1 Form

Form in the theatre

Form is the bedrock principle underlying *every* artwork, in whatever medium. It is its form that distinguishes an artwork from any other object that might be encountered in nature. Recent critical theory has perplexed many young artists by challenging the importance of *form* as an aesthetic necessity, but nothing more decisively differentiates artists from critics than the attitudes they can afford to indulge on the subject of form (especially so-called *literary* form, which differs fundamentally from *dramatic* form). In recent decades, several "lit-crit" schools of thought have quarreled with the term *formalism*, and thereby confused many young theatre artists about their proper professional preoccupation with *form* – a confusion that has led to some curious variations in *style*, but to no essential changes in dramatic form. What an academic critic means by moving somehow "beyond formalism," is very distantly related to what an artist must focus on while creating works of art. For an academic critic, moving beyond the straightjacket of any one *theory* about form might make some sense, but *form* itself is all that artists deal in. It is what defines their vocation, and it is a cruel illusion to imagine that art work can continue somehow *beyond* acquired expertise in form. In the theatre, form is as essential (and inevitable) as it is in painting, sculpture, architecture, music, poetry, or dance, but it eludes easy detection, and most people need to be trained to perceive dramatic form. The reason for this is that dramatic form is intangible and invisible; it can be grasped and remembered only with the mind.

The elusiveness of dramatic *form* is one of the baffling paradoxes of the theatre. The theatre is notorious for its vibrant, larger than life *presence*. How could all this manifest, "in-your-face" physicality and sensuous excess result in *forms* that are elusive? The theatre's glory (and frequently its shame) derives primarily from its exuberant *spectacle*; but it is precisely the *spectacle* – and all the immediacy of effect that spectacle suggests – that consistently misdirects our perception of dramatic *form*. The theatre is a hybrid art – some would say it is the only *complete* art – because it is simultaneously a visual art (within which all the creative means of painting, sculpture, and architecture are available) and a complex *performance* art (within which music, dance, and poetry can all find full expression). All the many spectacular dimensions of the theatre are meant to engraft themselves sensuously on our consciousness like experience itself. Dramatic *form*, however, is sculpted uniquely in time, and nothing is more elusive for the mind than "shapes" made in time by human artistry. We cannot even talk about them without recourse to analogies and metaphors (such as "shapes") drawn from other arts.

A first principle for artists, according to Lessing in his *Laocoön*, is that "*signs* that follow one another [in time] can express only *objects* whose wholes or parts are consecutive"; and furthermore, "objects or parts of objects which *follow* one another are called actions" (Lessing, 1984, p. 78). Thus poetry – an art of "articulated sounds in time" – necessarily deals with actions. On the stage, although there are bodies visually present,

> they also persist in time, and in each moment of their duration they may assume a different appearance or stand in a different combination. Each of these momentary appearances and combinations is the result of a preceding one and can be the cause of a subsequent one, which means that it can be *the center of an action*.
>
> (Ibid.)

Such purely formal observations are of enormous practical importance to composers in the time-arts, but they are clear only if one remains undistracted by "theme" or "content."

Form and content confusions

What is commonly meant by the "content" of a play is "whatever the play is about." *Story* is the term that dominates popular conceptions of the theatre and obscures a clear perception of dramatic form. Story is related to our second principle, action (the subject of Chapter 2), but it obscures a practical grasp of the first principle, form. A shift to analogies drawn from sculpture can help us wean the mind off "story" when thinking formally about a play. For a sculptor – let's say Michelangelo about to embark on creating the David – the "raw material" of his craft was a huge 18-foot block of quarried marble that had been lying in the "yard" of the Cathedral

Figure 1.1 Rough-hewn megalith of quarried marble and Michelangelo's David.
Source: Xpixel, Stock Photo; Jörg Bittner Unna, Creative Commons, CC BY-SA 3.0.

at Florence for over a generation (see Figure 1.1). This huge block of stone (nicknamed "the Giant") had been quarried and dragged down from the Carrara mountains with no clear idea how it would be used. From this matter, the young Michelangelo was to fashion one of the finest and best-known statues in Europe, the colossal David. What is the difference between these two pieces of stone, before and after the work of the sculptor? The rough-hewn monolith quite literally "contains" the finished David, and the finished David is missing only those portions of the original stone that *were not* the David – chips and shards of no value that it would have occurred to no one to save or preserve. The craft of the sculptor consisted quite simply (or *rien que ça*, as the French say) in chipping away from the big block all the extraneous stone that *was not* the statue of David.

Michelangelo left at his death a series of unfinished statues, most of them intended for the tomb of Pope Julius II (see Figure 1.2 "Captive Slaves"). These show figures emerging from half-sculpted stone and illustrate strikingly the gradual disclosure of recognizable forms from rough-hewn rock masses. Michelangelo himself stated in a poem (Michelangelo, 1991, p. 302):

Non ha l'ottimo artista alcun concetto
C'un marmo solo in sè non circoscriva
Col suo soverchio

(Not even the best of artists holds any concept
That a piece of raw marble does not already
Contain within itself)

(Author's translation)

It is an arresting insight into the nature of *form* and its relation to *content*. Is the finished David the "content" of the sculpture? The human form that results from the carving is surely the *formal* distinction between the two single blocks of marble (the unfinished and the finished sculpture). If the David were a play, however, we'd already be mired in "thematic" discussions of a different sort of "content," subjects like the Biblical David and his struggle with Goliath, or heroic nudity in pre-Christian Greece, or

Figure 1.2 Two of Michelangelo's "Captive Slaves."
Source: Jörg Bittner Unna, Creative Commons, CC BY-SA 3.0.

breaking sixteenth-century taboo in treating Biblical subjects, or the aux-
iliary "subjects" of defiant freedom of expression, of transgressive sexual-
ity, of racial typing, the idealization of males, or even extensions into the
general theme of anxiety and psychological stress. All of these are possible
"topics" associated with the "subject" of the work of art. In the case of a
sculpture, it is easier to return from such thematic excurses and stick
strictly to formal matters of craft; it is easier with the David to perceive the
important central fact that the final artistic product is *materially identical*
to the rough-hewn block of marble that was the artist's starting point.
Among sculptors, such craft-consciousness is all-important. What is the
formal equivalent to this simple craft perception in playwriting?

For a playwright, the formal equivalent to Michelangelo's huge block
of stone – the "raw material" delivered into his hands before he started
his formal work – is a chunk of time: say an hour or two of raw, unfash-
ioned time. *Three* hours is an outer limit verging on too much, and 4
hours is categorically too large a unit for a contemporary playwright to
work with. This *medium* (i.e., time) is a very difficult medium in which
to compose formal structures. How do you "carve" up time into artistic
forms? You do so through the time-arts of rhythm, tempo, duration, repetition, variation, legato, staccato, etc. These shapings of time units are
very far removed – conceptually– from *stories* and their typical thematic
preoccupations and associations. The shapes given to succeeding segments of time (durations) are properly referred to as the *plot* of a play.
Aristotle elaborated in *The Poetics* that what he meant by the *plot*
(μυθος) was "the arrangement of the incidents" (σύνθεσιν των
πραγμάτων), (Poetics 1450a, 4–5, in Butcher and Aristotle, 1951, p. 24)
and I follow his usage here.

Most people, when asked about the *plot* of a play (which should start
them thinking about a time-form) will start retelling the *story* they gath-
ered from attending or reading the play. Asked to describe the plot, most
people will fill us in on what they remember the play to have been about.
But "plot" is properly reserved to describe the *temporal form* of the play,
and developing the habit of perceiving the difference between plot and
story, or time-form and story "content" is the quickest way to develop
serious artistic consciousness in the theatre. The formal issue is complicated by the simple fact that most people who love the theatre are attracted
by what the theatre portrays (just as Michelangelo is widely appreciated
for his "lifelike" stone forms), and only secondarily by how the theatre
managed the portrayal of its so-called "content." Form is the most
important artistic aspect of the work of composition, and "content" is only
the pretext for building an artistic form – be it a stone-form in sculpture or
a plot-form in the theatre.

Time: the medium of the theatre

Since no play, in whatever style it was conceived, has ever escaped the necessity of unfolding in time, we can repeat Aristotle's ancient formal observation with reasonable confidence in its continued relevance: *all* plays necessarily have a discernible beginning, middle, and end. The defining time-medium is more intuitively obvious in the case of music and dance than it is in the theatre, where time-awareness is intentionally upstaged by spectacle. We will want, in practice, to continue to dazzle our audiences, but at some stage in training, theatre practitioners need to achieve active consciousness of *their* time-awareness. A simple way to grasp the difference is to consider how hard theatre artists work to assure that audiences are never "time-free" during a live performance. They are exposed to a relentlessly unfolding event in time – in fact it is common practice in the theatre to "push" the audience, to force-feed them at a pace that leaves them no leeway to wonder about other things, or wander in their own thoughts. There is a curious passage in Dante's *Purgatorio* that is relevant here. In Canto IV (line 10), the poet speaks of himself as losing track of time, and he muses on *"[la] potenza ... che l'ascolta"* – the faculty that "listens to" time. As theatre artists, we generally want complete control over the audience's "time-sense," or their faculty to perceive time itself as a medium. We are failing when they start looking at their watches. It is worthwhile pausing to consider what this "time faculty" is, and what it is that it is keeping track of.

Time is notoriously difficult to define. We might all agree with Saint Augustine, who left us in Book XI of his *Confessions* some of the best ruminations on time in our literature. He observed, "I know well enough what [time] is, provided that nobody asks me; but if I am asked what it is and try to explain, I am baffled" (Pine-Coffin and Saint Augustine, 1961, p. 264). Upon further reflection, Augustine noticed how long it was taking him to think through what time might be: "I have been talking of time for a long time, and this long time would not be a long time unless time had passed" (Sheed and Saint Augustine, 1943, p. 280). As still more time passed, Augustine puzzled on this intractably tautological quandary until he broke through to one of our most valuable insights about time perception:

> ... it is not the future that is long, for the future does not exist: a long future is merely a long expectation of the future; nor is the past long since the past does not exist: a long past is merely a long memory of the past..... The mind expects, attends and remembers: what it expects passes, by way of what it attends to, into what it remembers.
>
> (Ibid., p. 284)

And this observation is as good a description of the *medium* of the drama as any I have found anywhere. When we build dramatic performance "structures" out of time, we are building a sequence of durations, and these consist of effects attended to (by the audience) as they occur, then expectations born from these witnessed effects, and gradually an accumulating remembrance of the whole sequence – the "form" we properly call the "plot" of the play. In a *good* play, the time-sequence adds up to a memorable, distinguishable whole, with a clear beginning, a compelling middle, and a decisive and emphatic end.

Once we think of audiences using their memory and their innate "time-empathy" to "follow" and anticipate the course of a performance, we are thinking as a playwright or a director should. In the theatre, we make our artifacts primarily out of ongoing "units" of time. We contrive our packets of duration such that audiences are swept along by a time-form that is, we hope, under our artistic control. Audiences cannot stop the show for a second pass (unless we stage it such that they must); they do not have the freedom of another look, or a double-take with redoubled concentration. And this is the deepest principle of *form* in the drama. What you do with your time-form determines the *style* in which you practice. Robert Wilson, for instance, structures a great deal of extra time for audience reflection into his performances. That "extra" time is part of his *plot*. He also provides many occasions for a second look by re-staging recurrent motifs and figures. Because such staging breaks the by-now conventionally fast pace of performance, many people have found Wilson's stagings baffling at first sight, and "slow." But many who have secretly resented the coercion and artificiality of conventional staging have felt relieved and liberated attending Wilson's works. He has certainly freed them of the metronomic "ping-pong" exchange of conventional dialogue – something that alienates many people from the conventional theatre. He has also returned some of the *freedom* a coercive time-form curtails, letting the audience see – literally – in the "time-less" way Lessing described the experience of a viewer in an art gallery.

Duration

Duration is a word that describes the essentially *psychological* phenomenon isolated by Augustine: our innate ability to perceive passages of time as somehow "entities," something separable and portable (in our minds) as a "thing," a unit. The word "duration" is the name of this psychological experience of time. It contrasts, for instance, with the scientific postulate of an unbroken "flow" of time. It is routine for someone to ask a question like, "How long is the play?" and to receive a precise answer like,

"Two-and-a-half hours." Such an answer is an acknowledgment that duration is a commonplace perception. In our terms, that duration is the play's outer formal envelope. Within that whole, sub-units of time are variously strung together, and those will be what we sketch spatially as the "beads" when we draw a plot-bead diagram.

Duration (like "time") is not a particularly problematic word or idea until we try to pin it down and think about it seriously, as professionals must. When examined closely, duration becomes a bewilderingly elusive entity. It cannot be literally "seen" with our eyes, or "grasped" with the hands, but it is simultaneously the bedrock of our consciousness. We have invented, and we use all the time, "units" of duration as basic tools of our existence: seconds, minutes, hours, days, weeks, months, years, etc. Time itself has remained – long after Augustine grappled with the subject – one of the most baffling entities for philosophers, scientists, psychologists, and theologians to grasp and to define. For practical purposes in the theatre, we can locate the topic in the basic origins of duration and rhythm that are obviously lodged within our biological existence: our heartbeats are pretty clearly the example and source for our basic "small" unit of time, the second. Our breathing gives us a slightly longer (and very flexible) rhythmic unit that we exploit extensively in speech, singing, and chanting; walking gives us the *andante* tempo, and introduces all our "danceable" rhythms. Larger animals, primarily the horse, have given us the common rhythms and durations beyond human running and jumping: the third movements of Beethoven's symphonies, for example, are typically written in pronounced "horseback" rhythms.

As we continue to intuit sources for our units of duration, it is obvious that the daily passage of the sun "marks time" in a very concrete, visible way; in fact, our entire organism has evolved in deep congruence with the diurnal cycle: it is patterned into our organic being in the form of our digestive and metabolic "cycles." The moon's phases are the next perceptible unit of time; they have given us the duration measures of weeks and months. The seasons pattern in us a recognition of yet another scale of duration, and the year has been successfully perceived millennia before any understanding of the earth's orbit, or the tilt of the earth's axis could "explain" the recurring fact of the year cycle, which is deeply imprinted in the life of all vegetable matter. Death, of course, is the ultimate time-marker, and a human lifetime is the tacit duration "envelop" that compasses every use ever made of a theatre. An enormous number of plays end with a death scene – the ultimate formal *period*.

It is not hard, as we follow this progression, to sustain a workable idea of what sort of an "entity" is being brought up when we speak of duration. Philosophers, in fact, differentiate between what is technically a separable *entity* in the realm of thought and what is indivisible in human experience. Time may in fact be indivisible, but time-awareness in human life conjures symbolic representations or spatializations of this otherwise elusive subject by which we express an understanding of it. It will have escaped no thoughtful reader that this brief survey echoes what we know about the content, or themes, of the earliest cultural manifestations of the drama in ancient times. The very art of the drama was apparently invented to express or celebrate human awareness of periodic or cyclical phenomena. It was one of Aristotle's basic observations (in *The Poetics* and elsewhere) that an artist's preoccupation with time naturally expresses itself mimetically: performing artists use time to express their consciousness of time, and this is made clear in music, in dance, in recited poetry – all the "measured" arts; and these are – far from coincidentally – the ancestral arts which led to the invention of the drama.

Durations, or perceivable units of time, are our basic formal building blocks in the theatre. Of course, musical training is the best source of this lore for theatre students, but the plot-bead diagram is a device for formal "time-awareness" training and practice in the theatre.

A matter of hours

Duration brings up the topic of aesthetic scale, or the optimum perceptible *spans* of controlled time-form. Aristotle touched on this crucial aesthetic (and practical) problem in book vii of *The Poetics*. There he says (in S.H. Butcher's translation), "A beautiful object, whether it be a living organism *or any whole composed of parts*, must not only have an orderly arrangement of parts, but must also be of a certain magnitude." That *certain magnitude*, he went on to elaborate, is one "which can be embraced in one view" (Butcher, 1961, pp. 65–66). The analogy here is a visual one, but it is clear that theatres (*theatron* in Greek: the "seeing place") have been designed throughout the ages specifically to provide that embracing view for as many spectators as possible. That requirement alone (that everyone present be able to see the whole) dictates the architecture of *all* theatres, which resemble each other in every culture, in every historical period. To this day, the *location* of any seat in a theatre is valued by this one criterion made explicit by Aristotle: in the cheap seats, as everyone who has suffered in one knows, Aristotle's aesthetic criterion is not ideally realized.

In the case of a dramatic plot, the act of perception is a time perception, and we shift from the eye to that inner faculty "that listens to time," in Dante's phrase. The grasp of a *duration* is analogous to the seeing of a visual whole, and Aristotle was there attending to this crucial difference between media (it is probably here in *The Poetics* that Lessing gleaned the central thought for his *Laocoön*): "…in the *plot* [of a play], a certain *length* is necessary, and a length that can be easily embraced by the memory" (ibid., p. 66). On the topic of time, time-forms, and duration, Aristotle was on the same page in 350 B.C. that Augustine so laboriously reached in his *Confessions* some 600 years later. The observation is fully valid today: *a length that can be easily embraced by the memory* sets the scale for all the performing arts.

In practice most plays last from two to four hours. The point here is not to quibble over whether examples can be found to refute this general rule (remember that exceptions prove the rule) but to weigh the import of the fact that a play is always "a matter of hours." We may seem to be dealing with a needlessly theoretical topic here, but it is an intensely practical one in the theatre, one which governs innumerable discussions and decisions about play selection, play development, rehearsal planning, budgeting, performance, marketing, and audience response. In plain terms, a play that is "too long" (such as Robert Wilson's seven-days-and-seven-nights-long play *KA Mountain*) is an immense practical and aesthetic problem, and a play that is "too short" (such as Samuel Beckett's 40-second-long *Breath*) is also a production headache of questionable aesthetic value. Both cases raise serious dramaturgical problems about aesthetic scale, or the ability of a reasonable audience to perceive any intelligible form. In far less challenging cases, when plays-in-development are obviously too long or too short, the dramaturgical need to cut or lengthen the play requires ready practical knowledge of the basic principles of play construction, with a deep understanding of integrity of form, aesthetic wholeness, and the formal structures we build from an artful sequence of "durations."

Rituals of beginning and end

All well-run theatres train and rehearse elaborate customs of arrival, of greeting, of ticket-taking, of distribution of programs, of checking coats, finding and settling into seats. The conventions here are not without art: the audience is usually in the hands of trained staff as well as the theatre's architect, who has devised the theatre's interface with the street, something architects call "the lobby experience," and it includes elaborately contrived views, dramatic lighting, sound control, climate control – the elaborate creation of a sense of occasion. None of these things is irrelevant to the theatre experience, and few of them are usually left to pure chance. Most theatre architects lavish enormous amounts of care on the design of this "lobby experience," and theatre artists frequently feel competitive over this time during which a rival (the architect) has "our" audience to himself.

The beginning ritual intensifies as the appointed time comes nearer. As the house is filled, a natural crescendo of sound, the growing buzz of voices mutually exciting each other, generates an unmistakable anticipation of "The Beginning," a specific formal event. As that starting time approaches, music is often introduced to heighten the sense of impending occasion. When the time comes (our widespread convention is that the play begins ten minutes after the appointed hour, conceding a grace period for latecomers), the lights in the house fade, and this enormously dramatic blackout brings with it the expectation of silence in the house. This highly manipulative effect, incidentally, is a very recent formal capacity in the theatre, and it strikingly duplicates the awesome effect of dusk in nature, when the extinguishing of the daylight – swift and decisive daily event – automatically hushes and stills the daytime animals, just as it stimulates the nocturnal (and largely predatory) ones to activity. These analogies are not irrelevant to the modern theatre experience. In many European theatres, once silence is achieved in the house, the ancient custom of *les trois coups* (three loud blows struck with a heavy staff on the stage floor) announces the rising of the curtain and the formal beginning of the play. In America, curtains are now rare, and a general "lights up" on the stage signals that the play is officially beginning. This elaborately created occasion in time introduces the first segment of the plot (the first "bead" on the plot-bead diagram of the play), and "The Beginning" had better live up to the occasion created for it. Beginnings differ *formally* from "Middles" and "Ends," and looked at practically, this is a far from trivial observation. Artists in full control of the faculties of the drama will know just how to handle "Beginnings." Note that this is true regardless of theme, subject, period, or style of representation. This is a purely *formal* circumstance, created by manipulating time-consciousness in the minds of the audience: if successful we have created an *occasion*. Now to sustain and fulfill all it promises....

The point about time, duration, and form should by now be clear. It follows from these expositions that endings are equally conventional, equally important, and equally ritualized. When a play has come to an end, it is expected to create an unmistakable "sense of an ending." The curtain usually closes, or the lights fade one last time on the scene, and the audience then claps its hands (what a strange and wonderfully interactive custom!) while the actors, now by convention "out of character," return to the stage for a curtain call. A ballet of lights up, lights down, actors on, actors off, actors on again in new configurations, continues until a final exit and curtain, when the house lights signal that the audience is now expected to leave. Applause stops, and people leave their seats, retrieve their coats, and finally leave the building. The play is over. It stands to reason that this "thing" we so casually call "a play" is best grasped formally as an artful arrangement of events in time. The focus of the professional artist, it may seem strange to point out, must be on the skilled handling of that precious and concentrated "duration" that comes between the beginning and the end. With this consciousness of the literal nature of the task, we are mentally poised to take seriously the theoretical questions of dramatic form, and to learn the use of various formal tools. This craft is a major branch of dramaturgy.

The plot-bead diagram

The "plot-bead diagram," a visual device that charts the time-form of a theatrical plot, is drawn and named on analogy with a necklace: a sequence of individual beads (each representing a time-event) strung on a time-line in the order in which they occur in performance. The plot-bead diagram is a tool of analysis and an aid to swift mastery of form for directors and actors. As demonstrated in Figure 1.3 (discussed later in this chapter), it yields that "one view" of the otherwise elusive plot-form that all-too frequently evades detection in practice. It also greatly facilitates memorization of parts for performers, a secondary function I will discuss below. Directors of plays can be described as the custodians of *the formal cause.* Their specialization is to keep track of the *whole* while the individual performers make the parts. Experience has shown that actors in individual roles cannot perform this formal role well: they can't see the forest while they are busy being trees. It is impossibly hard, from *within* the structure, to see and shape the *wholeness* of the event. Conductors (usually, like directors, exempted from playing) have the same role in an orchestral ensemble; and the choreographer plays the same role in a dance troupe. But the whole form of a performance event is not easy to perceive, and once perceived, it is equally hard to hold firmly *as a whole* in one's mind in one act of intellection. A long and complex sequence of events in time boggles the average mind. People marvel, for instance, at musical maestros like the late George Szell, who routinely conducted large symphonic works without a score. Stage directors, conductors, and choreographers need to rise above average levels of perception to do their work. The plot-bead diagram is a device, a form of notation, for that formal grasp required of the custodians of the formal cause. It can serve as either a training device for learning *how* to perceive large performance structures (an hour or more in length) and it can continue to be useful as a permanent technique deeply integrated into a professional's work habits. Quite incidentally, the plot-bead diagram is also the best organizing principle for the correlative analytical work of the production dramaturg (see Chapter 3).

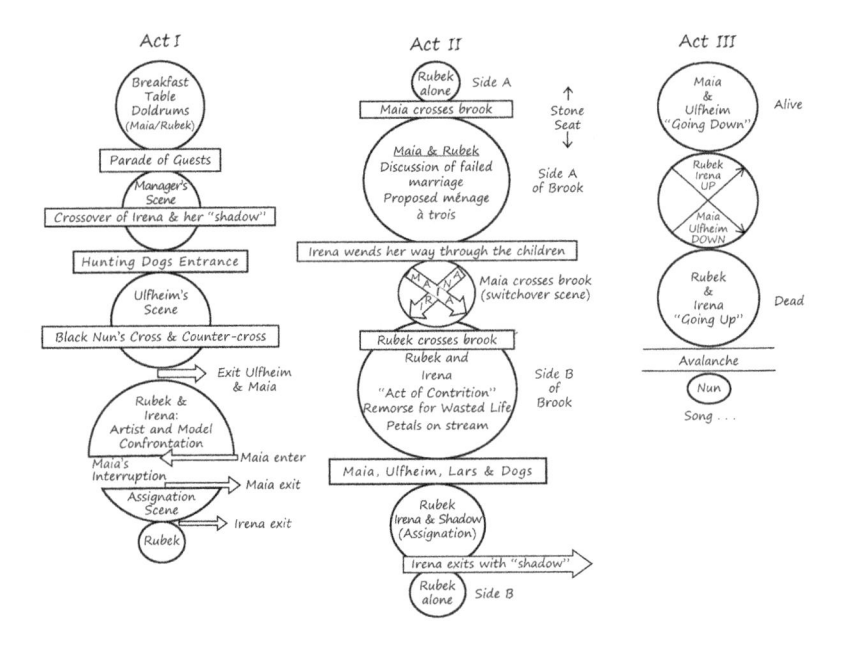

Figure 1.3 Plot-bead diagram of Henrik Ibsen's *When We Dead Awaken.*

Aristotle's proposition that the *sequence* of durations imitates an action can only be tested after we understand that all performance, whether good or bad, whether realistic of formalistic, whether organic and psychological or abstract and formal, whether it is "about" something, or whether it is defiantly "about" nothing (an impossibility, by the way), must still unfold in time – "one damn thing after the other." *All* performance forms can be sketched as plot-bead diagrams. In practice, one can't draw the plot-bead diagram of a play until one has analyzed the play, i.e., "cut it up" or "torn it apart" to isolate the individual "beads" for the diagram. The trick, of course, is to know what to call a "bead" or a "unit of duration" in making the plot-bead analysis. In the case of any particular play, we have to discern "what happens first," and this implies a direct perception of *when* something is "done." Then we must look for "what happens after *that*," and that in turn implies discerning when that *second* thing is "done"? And so on. There is, in fact, no other way to create a performance event. The objective behind the analysis is to have a very clear idea of what to do.

Act and scene divisions are a natural starting point for plot-bead break-downs, but they do not very often reveal the significant form of a play with enough finesse to be satisfactory. The ancient Greeks performed a highly ritualized sequence of choral songs (odes) interspersed with things *between* the odes (episodes). The Greek word *episode* has gradually come to be used as an equivalent for *scene*, but how do we know (especially if we are *composing* a scene) when a scene "ends"? And what are sub-units of *scenes?* The French have long used a rigorous system of sub-division that marks and numbers a new scene in a script whenever a character enters or exits; these divisions are known in English (somewhat disdainfully) as "French scenes," and though they are useful for the mechanics of rehearsal calls (what actors should show up when), they do not very often demarcate important *organic* divisions in a script. The Stanislavski System trained actors to look for "action beats" in individual scenes, and these can be marked out in any conventional play where characters interact via dialogue. But action beats, devised for individual actors, are generally also too small as units of division for a useful plot-bead diagram. So if French scenes and action beats chop things up *too* much, how do we get the analytical "units" just right? This question leads me to the analogy of the Wuhan chicken.

Chopped chicken vs. carved turkey

Stanislavski, in *An Actor Prepares*, gave an apt analogy for dividing an actor's part into "units": he compared it to carving a turkey. Stanislavski's point was that for the individual actor, the "whole turkey" could not be consumed in one bite, and that to be actable without being overwhelming, an actor's role had to be divided into manageable or bite-sized units of performance (Stanislavski, 1980, p. 111). Clearly, he was not pursuing the same principle of division we are seeking in order to make a useful plot diagram. Anyone who has had the disconcerting experience of being served chicken in a traditional Chinese setting (my exposure to this practice took place in a famous chicken restaurant in Wuhan – 1000 miles inland up the Yangtze River from Shanghai) will know that "bite-sized" need not bear any relation to anatomy. On the occasion in question, I was served a roasted and stewed bird that had been chopped up with a cleaver until all the pieces were of uniform smallness, and could be inserted into the mouth with chopsticks. But the blade of the cleaver had severed tendon meat and bone randomly, with resulting highly irregular fragments of shattered bone and integument intermixed with the meat one was meant to eat. For the diner in Wuhan, the rest of the operation takes place in the mouth, where the edible is separated from the jagged fragments of the inedible in a process of deft tongue, cheek, and jaw work that is not easy for the uninitiated. In fact, for those unable to achieve this, the process is dangerous. For the Chinese adept at this game, the process is fast and messy. Stripped remnants of carcass are ejected as the meal proceeds – and none too delicately. For me, there was blood drawn from tongue, gums, cheeks, and palate, and I quickly lost my appetite for the shreds of chicken available at such a cost. The process also violated my sense of aesthetics, which returns us to the subject at hand.

Because of its characteristically narrow focus on *acting*, Stanislavski's insight about carving the turkey stopped short of the useful formal information the plot-bead diagram is intended to yield up. One could divide a turkey into bite-sized chunks the Wuhan way, with no regard to organic structure (or what is otherwise called *anatomy*) and thereby achieve "manageable" without having bothered with any *formal* information at all. One can make a part *smaller* (and in that sense "manageable") by dividing it anywhere, but one analyzes its *formal structure* by dividing it at its distinctive organic joints – and these it takes a certain degree of discernment to find. That discernment is related to Action, as that will be detailed in the next chapter. Plot analysis, which might risk sounding dry and mechanical as it is detailed here, is really an art, not a science. It is an art completely analogous to the art of carving a turkey as it is usually practiced: the carver is expected to know, to sense, or to guess where the joints are so that when she cuts (the root meaning of analysis is to cut), she cuts significant parts away from each other. Robert Wilson, for instance, calls his formal dividers "knee plays" by analogy to the sort of organic anatomy I have been presenting here. Dramaturgical analysis of this kind is also an art that reveals its errors: a bad division doesn't work in the rehearsal hall, and it invites a revision. Usually a few minutes of rehearsal work on a difficult passage will re-center one's formal understanding. Once discerned, the organic parts become the strung "beads" of the diagram, and they should be drawn with flair – the diagram is a *drawing*, not a mathematical graph. In fact, plot-bead diagrams drawn too rigorously "to scale," with the beads strictly proportional to clock time or to pagination (or lineation) in the script, do not work. The *duration* in question is weighted by its psychological impact, by the emotional temperature of the scene, and the drawing should reflect these perceptual factors. Still, the most important aspect of the diagram is the *single view of the whole sequence that comprises the play*. Playscripts contain this information, but it is occulted by many factors, the dialogue and its ostensible subject matter being the worst offenders, the "story" being the next most distracting element. Dramatic form is far from apparent, even after many readings of a script.

Theatre and film share intimately the same deep formal architecture. In a film, the "plot-bead" structure of the whole is even more literally apparent than it is in a theatrical production. The final phase of composing a film is the assembly of the "final cut" in the editing room, and the spliced-together film is almost literally a "plot-bead" design: individual lengths of film, made directly proportional to a time-line by the sprockets that feed the film at a rigorously regular rate through the projector (thus providing the time-line of the film) are spliced one after another in a fixed sequence (the sequence of cuts) that is the "plot" of the film. This plot is completely analogous to the plot that governs the performance of a rehearsed play: this happens first, when that is done this happens after, then this, then this, and so on – until the last thing happens, and we signal the "end" of the film or play-structure. Films are composed on *exactly the same* formal principle as are plays, and *that* is the basis of their deep similarity. At the formal level, you can train for theatre or film with the same underlying principles of dramaturgy. But at any step above this level, the two media diverge wildly. In neither case, however, does it do any good to confuse *plot* with *story* – one of the most egregious habitual faults of the Hollywood film industry.

Case study 1: Julius Caesar, Act IV, Scenes ii and iii

Shakespeare composed in scenes: they are the basic units of his dramaturgy. The folio of 1623 divided and numbered scenes according to "continuous action" criteria: a scene does not end until a break in dramatic action is made (a "jump-cut" to use anachronistic but appropriate film terminology). But sometimes dividing scenes by the sole criterion of whether or not the action remains continuous hides subtle articulations into secondary scenes, and sometimes into tri-partite divisions or more – all without a formal break in the action. Such modulation is a mark of supreme dramaturgical skill, and Shakespeare is (as in all else) our exemplary master of such "sub-scene" technique. The complex sequences he often builds, while still demarcated as one scene, form powerful sub-structures within the plot of his plays, dramatic forms that might be called *movements*, or *passages* – the terminology being less important than a clear grasp of the specific *forms* such words attempt to designate. The plot-bead diagram elucidates such forms by drawing a graph of what happens first, what happens next, what happens after that – rigorously charting the exact *sequence* that builds the form. In *Julius Caesar* there is a memorable passage of this kind in Act IV, just before the decisive dénouement of Act V (the battle of Philippi). The full passage, which spans two marked scenes, is illustrated in the plot-bead diagram of Figure 1.4.

The movement in question is an amazing piece of dramaturgy focused on the state of the rebel leaders, principally Brutus and Cassius, one night shortly before their destruction at Philippi. The sequence begins with a

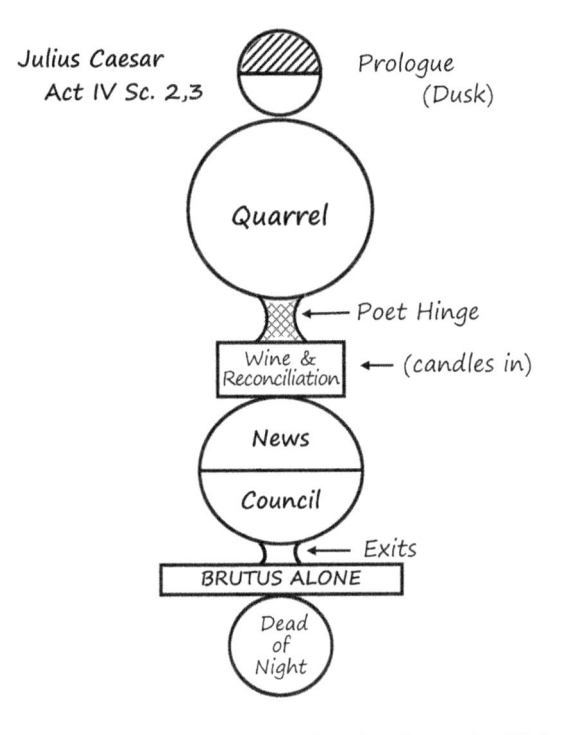

Figure 1.4 Plot-bead diagram of Shakespeare's *Julius Caesar* Act IV, Scenes ii–iii.

brief outdoor scene (IV, ii) in which Brutus, at the head of his army, calls a halt to its march and is soon joined by Cassius, who has led his own contingent to the same halting place (in a film, they might be shown on horseback in this prologue). The two commanders have a quarrel to settle, and choose not to pursue it in the open before their troops. Their decision to retire into Brutus' tent leads to a scene break, and IV, ii therefore ends and IV, iii begins according to the convention of folio divisions. Note that the two principal actors who must exit from the stage to end scene ii (Brutus and Cassius) are the same two actors who must enter to begin scene iii. Such an arrangement is usually considered a flaw in play construction, but here its justification is organic to the action. So much for "rules" of composition (though the principle of avoiding such come-and-go remains valid)! A director who has done his structural homework will engineer some solution to this awkward juncture between scenes; the fluency of modern staging makes it easy for a director to run the scenes together without an acting break, for instance by swirling in a scene change (in this case a tent) rather than sending two angry characters off-stage only to have them absurdly re-appear angrier still with no intervening action. In any case, what the script calls scene ii clearly functions as a prelude to the whole movement of the complex scene iii.

In a large overview of the whole play (like Figure 1.3 of *When We Dead Awaken*) one might be tempted to assign just one "bead" to each of Shakespeare's scenes, but that would miss a deeper structure crafted into this passage of the play. Scene iii contains at least four major segments worthy of successive "beads" on the diagram – it is, in fact, four *scene units* in a row, with three "continuous action" hinges bridging the scene elements. The whole chain of seven segments (a number arrived at by adding the hinges to the scenes) is played with no break in acting continuity. The total sequence will have eight segments if one chooses to incorporate the prologue as suggested above. This, incidentally, makes the passage in question a *tour-de-force* for the actor playing Brutus, who remains at the eye of the dramatic storm without a break for some half-hour (or more, depending on the tempi) of uninterrupted acting. For the actors, each of the seven "units" of scene iii (four "beads" and three "hinges") can and must be carefully sub-divided into yet smaller significant parts. In theory, this formal sub-division continues down to individual speeches or "lines" (the usual level at which the untutored or inexperienced actor approaches a script) and – since this play is written in verse – to individual poetic lines, metrical feet, words, syllables, and phonemes. This may sound absurd, but in Shakespeare productions, careful analysis and drilling in vocal sound *at this level* is also a required art. Vocal coaches and verse experts are routinely called in to drill inexperienced actors until they acquire the necessary "classical" technique to handle Shakespearean verse. And the trained "classical" actor spends hours parsing, pronouncing, and repeating aloud every fragment of his vocal part, until the physical choreography of the speaking apparatus (lips, teeth, jaw, tongue, palate, esophagus, vocal chords, lungs, and diaphragm) has been drilled into a *physical* memory as rigorous as that of dancers drilled to performance pitch.

But to return to scene iii: the first of the four big divisions (after the prologue) is the furious quarrel that explodes between the commanders – something that showed signs of beginning "outside" in scene ii, but was adjourned to the relative privacy of Brutus' tent. This is a stunning scene of fury that begins at high pitch and rises higher as two major figures dispute a central accusation (Cassius' alleged cupidity). It is magnificently written, both for its energy and psychological discernment and for its high rhetoric, diction, and perfect repartee. It goes on page after page as the two co-conspirators rage on, and it ends only after Cassius breaks and falters, an important psychological moment to pinpoint in rehearsal (I would place it provisionally at line 55 – but such things are settled in each production in the rehearsal hall, where the full dynamic of the action is a reality in front of our eyes). Wherever Cassius breaks, the whole scene is one bead on the diagram. As they spend their energy, the two antagonists are interrupted by one of the most curious scenelets in Shakespeare – and one usually cut in performance – the intrusion of a nameless poet (who appears only here). Only 15 lines long (the quarrel scene is 122 lines long) the poet's scene breaks the flow only to deliver a single, bad, rhyming couplet which is a doggerel platitude about patching up quarrels. Why stop the play to insert this? The answer is that the poet's interruption functions as a "hinge" into a next segment of the play. All plays are made this way: the ongoing sequence alternates between major scenes and connecting devices that can variously be called "hinges" or "transitions" or "joints" or "knees" (the last the term favored by Robert Wilson). Hinges negotiate a structural transition between temporal parts; their presence in plays is really proof of the inherent plot-bead structure we are sketching. Interruptions are invariably "hinges," for *by definition* they bring something to a halt and force "something else" to replace it. Playwrights use hinges in telling ways, and here, Shakespeare brings this "poet" in from left field at a point in the scene when the main energy has spent itself, and the scene really is "over," yet he doesn't want an exit. While getting the intruding poet expelled, Cassius "sets up" the next big scene by asking that Messala be brought to Brutus' tent. A lot of traffic management, backstage instruction, and plot arrangement takes place: who *is* that obtruding poet? Can it be Shakespeare mocking his own exposed hand as he manipulates the plot?

The interruption triggers a reconciliation – the next bead on the diagram – during which Brutus orders wine, and while waiting for it to come, reveals that his wife Portia has recently committed suicide. This devastating news now colors the previous scene in retrospect – as Cassius immediately realizes – and he seizes on this to restore and cement his good relations with Brutus. The men are tense, exhausted, and emotionally drained by the time they drink their wine pledge, and Messala's arrival (accompanied by one Titinius, a character who remains silent and is therefore often deleted in production) provides the hinge into the next significant plot bead. Note that this hinge was set up in the previous hinge, when Cassius sent for Messala, but his actual arrival – something completely within the control of the dramatist – coincides with the completion of an action beat (the reconciliation). Though hinges always have a purely structural function, they are also always a dramatic opportunity for punctuation or counterpoint. Here Shakespeare re-enforces the "closure" of the reconciliation by the timing of the arrival. With the new characters onstage, the third major segment of scene iii begins (bead 4 on the diagram).

This bead is best described as the Council of War. Like many scenes in Shakespeare, it has a two-part structure. First, news is pooled as a preliminary for a war council, then the council is held and a decision reached. This follows the plot structure of almost *every* executive meeting, not only in Shakespeare's plays, where there are innumerable court scenes, with regents or generals tending to present business, but also in typical examples from contemporary life: meetings typically are governed in time by an agenda, and an agenda is a plot-bead diagram for a meeting. The news assembled in Brutus' tent is not good. Octavius Caesar and Marc Antony are at the head of a mighty army, and a terrible number of their fellow senators – between 70 and 100, including Cicero – have been executed as traitors. It is hard not to pause at each segment to suck the marrow from this rich play. That will be one of the tasks of full Production Dramaturgy, as outlined in Chapter 3, but for our present purposes suffice it to say the War Council "bead" ends unambiguously when Brutus asks, "There is no more to say?" and Cassius answers, "No more. Good-night." At that juncture, another hinge begins: a general exit beat full of farewells and valedictums, ending in a cascading chorus of "goodnights" which is a trademark in Shakespearean dramaturgy.

At this point, Shakespeare might well have stopped and ended Act IV, but instead he wrote on, and the epilogue, or coda he composed in this place is one of the most beautiful *rhythmic* compositions in his whole canon. No necessity is driving the dramaturgy here, only the free play of the inner instincts of a composer of genius. One is tempted to guess that, having so deeply evoked and tracked the inner life of his Brutus to this point, he was just unable to let him go. I have called the final bead in the diagram the Dead of Night coda, and for purposes of a plot-bead diagram, this is good enough. However, the coda itself is worth analyzing in meticulous detail (see Figure 1.5), for it reveals in a small figure the whole principle of sculpting in time-form that the plot-bead analysis helps us to grasp and to appreciate. If this were a passage in a Beethoven piano trio, or a string quartet (the ending of one of the slow movements, for instance) we could not do it justice in performance without a detailed mastery of its *form*, and careful calibration of its rhythm and tempo in performance. The same is true of this exquisite coda at the end of Act IV of *Julius Caesar*.

The coda begins with a stage direction that hides a powerful theatrical effect: *Exeunt all but Brutus*. Leaving this protagonist alone on the stage, isolated in the light of a single taper – after all we have heard and seen – can be in itself a theatrical *coup* if well handled. Such isolation and silence can last a good while in performance, and its impact can warrant a distinct place-marker on a chart of our time-beads. As we will soon see, this tableau of isolation and silence might well be repeated at the end of the

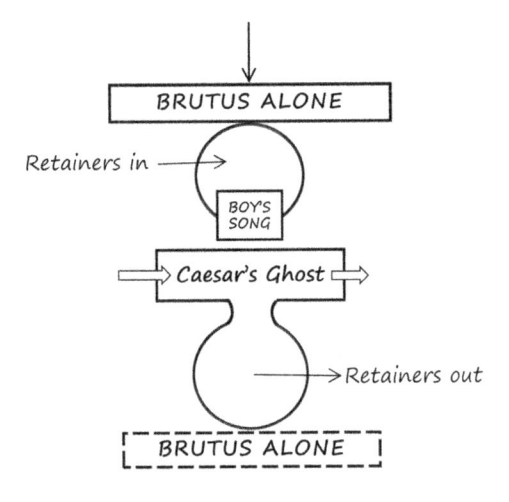

Figure 1.5 Detailed plot-bead diagram of the "Dead of Night" Coda, *Julius Caesar* Act IV, Scene iii.

coda, re-enforcing the sense that the act *could* have ended here. But Shakespeare has Brutus' bone-weary boy servant appear with his master's nightgown, and the coda is launched when Brutus, as he changes into nightclothes, asks the exhausted boy if his musical instrument is near at hand.

Cued by the boy's evident need for sleep at this late hour, Brutus changes his mind and asks for two retainers to be called into the tent. They come at once and are told to make themselves comfortable on the floor and to sleep there in case they need to be dispatched on urgent business. Clearly, Brutus cannot face sleep without company. The protesting retainers do as they are told, and Brutus suddenly finds a book he had mislaid in the pocket of his gown. He apologizes to his boy, who had evidently been accused of mislaying it, then asks the boy to play a little music after all. The drowsy boy readily agrees, in an exchange of such exquisite tenderness between master and servant that the tone and pace suggest the extenuated largo and pianissimo of the Beethoven analogies hinted at above.

The next small figure is the boy's song, during which he, and presumably the two retainers sprawled on the floor, fall asleep. Alone again in the dead of night, Brutus broods on the sleeping boy, and again with excruciating tenderness and delicacy, extricates the boy's instrument from his sleeping form. The dramaturgy has brought us rhythmically, by lapped cadences, to the stillest of still points, a purely *rhythmical* imitation of "the dead of night." Brutus remembers his book, and as he strives to find his place in it to read, his candle suddenly falters as it burns (a great cue for modern lighting effects) and the slaughtered Caesar's ghost appears in the tent. There could be no better school than this for learning how to orchestrate a *coup de théâtre*. The ghost, having scored his effect mainly by showing up, says little (three short lines) and leaves soon, but the scene of horror is the principal *raison d'être* for the coda. Brutus endures it as he has endured everything else throughout this act: with iron self-control and stoic dignity. After the ghost exits, an almost exact bookending of the sequence that led step by step to the ghost's appearance disassembles the scene. First the boy is awakened and quizzed on whether he has seen anything (a curious question to ask one evidently sound asleep), then the two retainers are shaken awake, asked the same absurd question, and sent in distracted haste to Cassius with the vague mission of urging him to an early start. The script of *Julius Caesar* specifies no further continuation to the scene, but it is hard, with modern scenic technique at our disposal, to resist completing the symmetry revealed by the plot-bead diagram: the whole structure of the dramaturgy suggests closing the scene not with the general hurried exit required by Elizabethan stage conditions, but with a bookend: a still tableau of the almost empty stage, with Brutus alone with his sleeping groom, keeping sleepless vigil as his candle flickers and burns.

A final observation about time is in order after this example of a plot analysis, which charts the dramaturgical arrangement of incidents in time. Though the whole passage here isolated plays unambiguously, in front of our eyes, in "continuous time," it portrays in the *story* a good deal more time than actually elapses in the plot. I estimate the passage to have a playing time of roughly 30 minutes, but even though it never "stops" or cuts away (to use film terms) it portrays a span that starts at latest at dusk, and ends most plausibly at midnight, if not later. Thus, story time has been compressed under our very noses, and an unbroken 30 minutes or so of performance time has "represented" at least 6 hours of story time. This paradox is everyday thaumaturgy for those who work in the theatre, and critics with a purely literary orientation fail to grasp that the effect *derives* from the profound aesthetic difference between plot and story.

Case study 2: Robert Wilson's *Einstein on the Beach*

Plot-bead diagrams can be drawn of *any* performance event, even unscripted "happenings," if someone keeps a record of what happened. If the event is to be a *repeatable* one (the usual situation in the theatre), the chart of "things you do" will have practical utility as well as being analytically illuminating. Sequence charts are often posted in green rooms and dressing rooms so that offstage actors can refer to them swiftly and assess at a glance "where they are" in the time-progress of a play. These are rudimentary plot-structure diagrams. There is no high aesthetic aim to such charts, just the practical objective of getting actors onstage on cue, but their presence does reflect the higher aesthetic truth that missed entrances devastatingly *disrupt* the plot-form of a play. The plots of all performance events can be charted, no matter what the style, no matter what the setting, and what the conditions of performance might be. In all cases, the sequence is the plot, and manipulating the sequence – artfully inventing and arranging the plot – is a master key to one's deepest action as a composer for the stage.

Robert Wilson, after the sensational success of his postmodern opera, *Einstein on the Beach* (premiered July, 1976, at the Avignon Festival), was forced by his success to make public appearances and to speak discursively at symposia and lecture/discussions about his methods in the theatre. At first, he hated doing this, but over the decades since *Einstein*, he has acceded to the frequent requests to be seen and to speak about the artistic methods behind his compositions for the stage, and he has now gotten very good at performing set lectures about his craft. Immediately after *Einstein on the Beach*, audiences at symposia wanted to hear explanations of the content of the enigmatic opera. They were visibly baffled when Wilson, at that time reluctant to talk at all, outlined his procedural plan for composing *Einstein on the Beach*. He drew on a chalkboard at one such symposium (at Harvard in 1985) a dry sketch that I reproduce from my notes below.

Robert Wilson's plot outline of *Einstein on the Beach*

O
I a
b
O
II c
a
O
III b
c
O
IV a
b
c
O

He explained how he chose before anything else the relative *duration* of the segments of the performance he envisioned. He chose the number of "parts" in each segment and *their* desired durations, then arranged them in a permuted sequence of simple mathematical design based on repeated patterns of threes. Thus, there were nine initial durations planned for *Einstein on the Beach*: three sets of three, or "motifs" a, b, and c repeated three times, then further sub-divided into a "four-act" structure as shown in his structural outline. Five "knee plays" – designated by the large Os in the outline – were added, for a total of 14 consecutive segments. Only after thus designing his plot did Wilson move on to back-filling these formal elements with "content." Motif "a" was to be his "Train" motif, "b" his "Trial" motif, and "c" his "Spaceship" motif. His audience at the lecture in the 1980s was bewildered, with many bright people in attendance openly grumbling about artistic fraud and deliberate obfuscation. To many, the dry presentation of the formal tectonics of an already baffling composition just confirmed their sense that an *avant-garde* flim-flam man was thumbing his nose at them. Wilson's laconic, tongue-tied manner, both aloof and detached, did not soften this impression. But he was presenting very clear information about the plot of *Einstein on the Beach* in purely formal terms, and he hadn't the slightest instinct to hide or misrepresent his procedures. Wilson is unique among American theatre artists in composing formal plots directly for the stage, with only secondary attention paid to the "matter" within these formal plots. He is completely oblivious to the insistent conventional demand for discernible "story" logic, or some anecdotal "hook" that can help audiences follow the thread of an expected response. Wilson does not traffic in conventional cues for audience response, but he expects (and anticipates) the audience's response in his every move. He expends enormous energy and concentration on every presented detail and the *placement* in time of each detail. Almost nothing is "random" in a Wilson work – on the contrary, there is far less temporal ad libbing in his theatre than there is in the everyday fare of "realist" productions, which are downright sloppy by comparison.

In the final version of *Einstein on the Beach*, Wilson augmented his nine-scene plot structure with five knee plays placed before each act and after the last. He further sub-divided Act I, Scene 1 by making *it* a distinct three-part structure – the parts divided by abrupt blackouts – as though he wanted to introduce the *theme* of threes at the outset of this long opera. Philip Glass took Wilson's triple repeat form in Act I, Scene 1 as his cue to establish his three principal musical motifs in that first scene. As finally performed, *Einstein on the Beach* had 14 major "beads" on a plot-bead diagram (the nine scenes plus the five knee plays), with the first bead a tiny trinity-figure in its own right. Figure 1.6 illustrates this structure of the

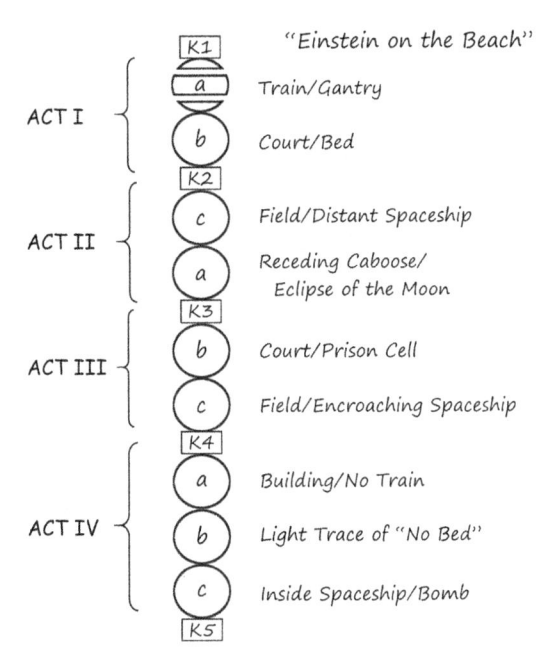

K1 "Einstein on the Beach"

ACT I

a Train/Gantry

b Court/Bed

K2

ACT II

c Field/Distant Spaceship

a Receding Caboose/ Eclipse of the Moon

K3

ACT III

b Court/Prison Cell

c Field/Encroaching Spaceship

K4

ACT IV

a Building/No Train

b Light Trace of "No Bed"

c Inside Spaceship/Bomb

K5

Figure 1.6 Basic plot-bead diagram of Robert Wilson's *Einstein on the Beach.*

opera. What becomes striking as one studies this One View of the whole structure, is that each "part" is governed by a binary opposition of its own, and these are labeled in the plot-bead diagram. The knee plays are likewise all antiphonal duets, in each case small-scale personal "figures" juxtaposing the black performer Sheryl Sutton to the white dancer Lucinda Childs. Within the order of the plot-bead diagram it is possible to see a progression through each motif, something otherwise difficult to grasp at any one performance. The three train sequences trace the vanishing of this nineteenth-century mode of transportation (and of the industrial world it supported), the Trial sequences trace the disappearance of the large bed at the center of the courtroom, and the awful encroachment of the prison cell (in what could be seen as a visual correlative to the socio-historical theories of Michel Foucault), and the three Spaceship sequences trace a gradual crowding of human dancers in an open field – one that ultimately swallows the dancers up inside an imprisoning spaceship which explodes in nuclear annihilation. Things become startlingly clear, or at least thematically legible, at this level of analysis, but the point is not to explain or de-mystify the many meanings of *Einstein on the Beach* (something which can be done quite convincingly by following the lead I have just thrown out), but to better appreciate the formal *event* so unforgettably placed before us in this masterwork.

Wilson himself always composes with plot-bead diagrams of his own – in fact he sketches *all* his ideas, the way other people *talk* all the time. His preferred drawing style differs, however, in that he sets up storyboard frames that sequence out the plot in visual terms. See Figure 1.7, his sketch of the 14 boxes of *Einstein* (from Shyer, 1989, p. 219). His boxes are pro-scenium frame views of the dominant geometry of each scene, so their primary shorthand is spatial, not temporal. Still, Wilson arranges these spatial views in a temporal sequence that has the same form and objective as does a plot-bead diagram: to give the whole *performance form* in one view. Wilson's scene–frame storyboards sum up synoptically the totality of the *dramatic* composition, while simultaneously recapitulating the

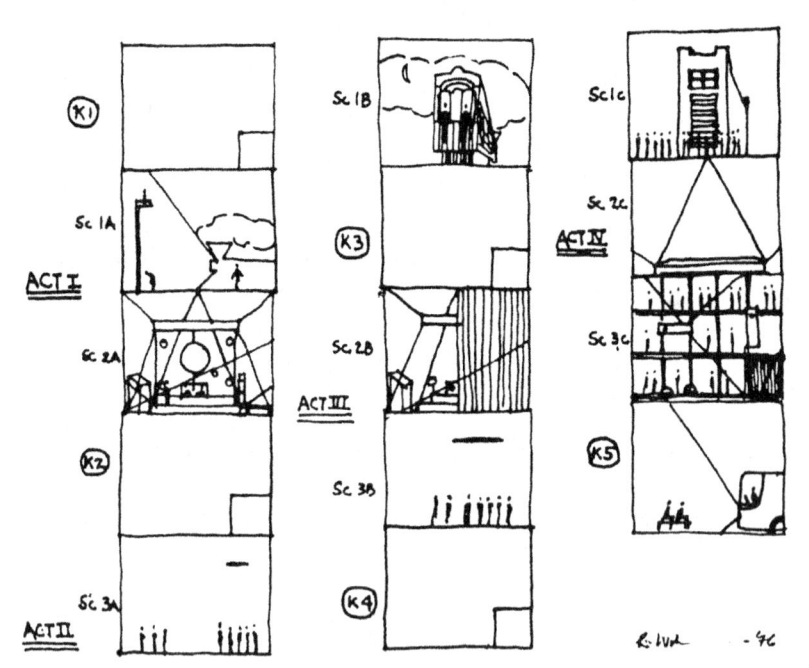

Figure 1.7 Robert Wilson's storyboard sketch for *Einstein on the Beach.*
Source: Robert Wilson/RW Work, Ltd.

"look" of each scene. They are, in effect, "flash frames" that jump us part by part through time. They are meant to be read *syntactically* as a time progression, the way we read the strung meaning of a sentence on a page.

The fact that Wilson's explanatory graphics and frank descriptions of his artistic procedure irritated so many Americans (and, at that same date, irritated far fewer Europeans) attests to the enormous cultural aversion Americans have to purely formal matters in theatre arts. In the world of music and music composition, such procedures are far more commonplace, and the general culture among musicians (whose formal training is much more rigorous than is that of theatre artists) permits open discussion and conscious appreciation of intricate formal exercises in ordering and permutating durations. No one feels that "creativity" is being compromised in the process. *Einstein on the Beach* is of course a collaboration between Wilson's stagecraft and Philip Glass's breakthrough musical score, so it was, in fact, a musical event as much as it was a visual and theatrical one. It is probably because of the music that the show succeeded so spectacularly in winning an American audience, and indeed, it was the New York music critics (John Rockwell prominent among them) who first hailed the opera as a major work. Philip Glass's collaboration began at the plot-stage I have outlined above, and Glass's explanation of the project makes the time-sculpting very clear (Shyer, 1989, p. 220):

> What we're doing is taking two three-part structures and spreading them over three two-part structures. Consider for the moment the first three acts – each of those acts is in two sections (sc. 1, 2) and against that I'm putting two three-part structures (1-2-3, 1-2-3). That's something we do in music all the time. The fourth act is 1-2-3 all together – it's actually a recap of the first three acts. What we have is a musical idea that works as a dramatic idea… it gave us a common structure.

Anyone who listens to the Glass score of *Einstein on the Beach* can hear the threes and twos beating rhythmically against each other. Rhythm is a constitutive plot device in the theatre just as much as it is in music, and it operates as a principle of composition across the entire spectrum of the human attention span.

It is best to avoid "theme" topics while mastering any formal structure, but that is only an injunction meant to focus one's work in the theatre and make it more efficient. It is not to be confused with a principle of criticism, or explanation. This is one important way in which dramaturgy differs from criticism. *Einstein on the Beach* is loaded with themes, and those themes develop and converge in a dramatic climax that is both analyzable and significant (and a significant factor in people's appreciation of the opera). It would be wrong to imply that this "content" is not put there by Wilson, or that it isn't meant to be apparent. But *interpreting* those themes, or explicating *meanings* in works like *Einstein on the Beach* is not a good objective for the performing artists *in* the work. It *can* be done, but doing so yields very little leverage on the power of the work in performance. This is as true in formalist works like Wilson's as it is in conventional works with stories to tell and issues to air, but the latter styles of drama (styles closer to Realism) suffer from a lack of just such formal attention as Wilson lavishes on his more abstract work. By contrast, if one hopes to re-stage *Einstein*, (or any of Wilson's works) one needs huge amounts of carefully organized formal information: "production books" where convention would posit "playscripts." Wilson works with dedicated stage managers and stage assistants (including dramaturgs) who meticulously document this formal information for each production. In the course of doing so, these formal custodians develop a very powerful sense of the "meaning" of the work, but they are seldom called upon to document this *meaning* by making it explicit. Most of us who have been in this position are furthermore reluctant to *reduce* his magnificent theatre compositions to mere descriptions of meaning. This does not mean the meanings are not there.

I watched Wilson stage three productions at the American Repertory Theatre subsequent to *Einstein*: The Köln section of *the CIVIL warS* (1985), Euripides' *Alcestis*, with a parallel text by Heiner Müller (1986), and Müller's *Quartet*, a deliberately perverse condensation of Choderlos de Laclos' *Les Liaisons Dangereuses* (1988). When Wilson returned in 1991 to stage Ibsen's last play, *When We Dead Awaken* (a neglected play often considered unstageable), I served as his production dramaturg. We started our work with a plot-bead diagram (Figure 1.3 above), which Wilson found far more interesting than the traditional detailed "reading" of the play outlining its themes and story-line. With the diagram before him, he "sketched in" his treatment of each of the "beads" on the diagram, and used the suggestive horizontal crossovers as major dividing "passages" by which to measure out our progress through the first act of the play. By the time I worked with Wilson, I had worked closely with David Warrilow, who was himself "Wilsonized" when he performed in *The Golden Windows* at the Brooklyn Academy of Music in 1985. David and I understood clearly from our common work with Samuel Beckett that the tighter the control of form by the composer/director, the greater the inner freedom of the performer – and this guided me in focusing on *formal* information to assist Wilson's staging of *When We Dead Awaken*.

Wilson is supremely uninterested in conventional dramaturgy, but what he *is* interested in is still dramaturgy: the construction of beautiful, staged time-events. For these, he needs a plot, and if given a "conventional" play script, he wants to convert it as soon as possible into a plot-form that will guide his composition in time and space. "Structure gives me freedom," he said at a lecture at Harvard in February, 2000. Most of the supposed aesthetic "problems" of his theatre can be settled by accepting the fact that he is the new author of the eventual piece. Traditionally (and legally), a playwright is the formal "author," but Wilson typically assumes a usurping authority over other people's plots; in the case of *When We Dead Awaken* he remained remarkably true to Ibsen's visionary plot – so much so that I, for one, became convinced that Wilson "realized" Ibsen's last play better than Ibsen himself had been able to do, hobbled as he was by the conventions of his century. Yet the "unstageable" plot-form was the surviving clue that Ibsen managed to leave behind, and it "contained" the essence of a poetic vision of astonishing power. To say that the Wilson staging of the play "depicted" a man's passage out of life and into death, is a bathetic *reduction* of an aesthetic event too rich to paraphrase and too complex to describe with discursive language alone. Every play and every production should aim as high, but none can reach such heights without consummate formal architecture.

Case study 3: Samuel Beckett's *Rough for Theatre II*

As a final example illustrating plot-bead diagrams, or drawings of the time-form, let me turn to a small, relatively minor play by Samuel Beckett, the playlet he published under the non-title of *Rough for Theatre II*. The play is only 19 pages long in its printed form in the Grove Press edition of 1976 (Beckett, 1976, pp. 93–112), but it plots out to a distinctive shape in time (Figure 1.8), with roughly 20 small plot beads that group into four main parts: three distinct *movements* and a coda. To re-iterate, there is no play, from any period, in any style, which does not generate a plot-bead diagram. But plots vary considerably in their formal coherence, and the "meaning" contained in their form. This example illustrates well the stark difference between plot and so-called "story" content. Beckett was a meticulous craftsman of play-forms, and his characteristic artistic signature is startling form/content disparities such as the one he devised here. The little theatrical sketch (or "rough" as he called it) he contrived is really a masking device for unbearable pain, the "subject" of this exercise. The pain, however, is largely *generated* by the disparity between form and content. The *form* of *Rough for Theatre II* is four-square, self-evident, and forceful, while the pitiful *content* – mute, and still and quasi-catatonic – withers by contrast into despairing insignificance. The play is "about" an impending suicide – and one that doesn't happen, at that – at least not

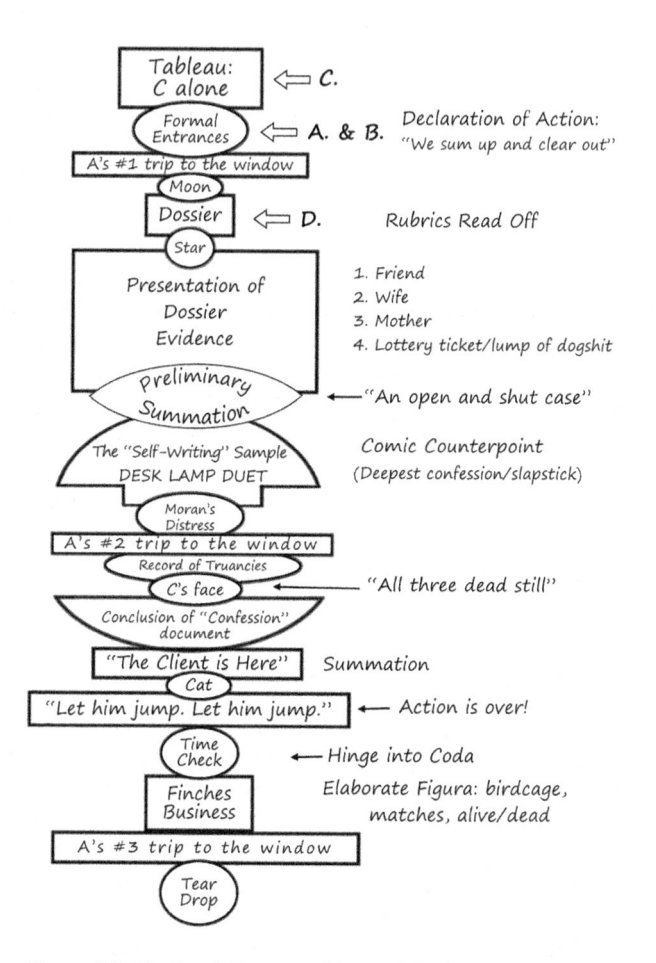

Figure 1.8 Plot-bead diagram of Samuel Beckett's *Rough for Theatre II.*

while we attend. But let's look closely at the form and "read" the arrangement of the incidents – or Aristotle's σύνθεσιν των πραγμάτων.

The play begins with a symmetrical tableau: a central window upstage center, two facing desks with chairs downstage right and left, each dressed with a plain desklamp. We are in a "room." As our eyes adjust to the dimly lit space, we notice a silent figure standing at the window ledge, his back to the audience: this figure is identified by Beckett as "C." As we will discover in the course of the play, "C" is the protagonist of the piece, and he neither moves nor speaks throughout the play. The first "bead" on our plot diagram is the "playing" of this tableau, in silence, without motion or sound.

Tableaux are frequent stage devices, and very effective as plot beads. This opening bead is soon followed by an entrance sequence: first one character (identified laconically by Beckett as "A") enters from a door on stage right, crosses the stage, and sits at the stage left desk; then another character ("B") enters and takes the symmetrical seat at the desk on stage right. The full stage picture is thus composed in this second plot sequence, and the full cast (as it turns out) is assembled. Each of the two newcomers turns his desk lamp on, clearly indicating a beginning. There will be no more actors involved in the play.

We notice toward the end of the "formal entrances" segment of the play (bead two in the diagram) that preset at B's desk was a briefcase containing a dossier of folders and documents. As B unpacks and prepares to deal with these documents, A closes the "formal entrances" segment of the plot with a concise statement of the intended action: "We sum up and clear out." Playwrights who knew what they were doing when they constructed their plays have frequently left clear, explicit action statements in their opening plot beads, as Shakespeare did in *Measure for Measure* when the Duke says, "Of government the properties to unfold." We can learn to sense a "hinge" between beads by looking for exchanges of the sort that follows:

A: Set to go?
B: Rearing.
A: We attend.

This starts another plot bead. B opens the new plot segment by stating his conclusion: "Let him jump." This pronouncement launches the *story*-subject in the minds of the spectators. C is – we quickly realize – a potential jumper contemplating suicide. In this bead, A makes the first of what will be three trips to the jumper's window. The plot-bead diagram makes it clear that the three trips mark off the play's time-form very precisely, marking (in good Aristotelian fashion) the beginning, the exact middle, and the end.

Upon his return to his desk, A remarks that he noticed a full moon in the evening sky. A quick exchange with B leads to the consultation of an almanac, and the realization that this evening is the close of the Feast of Our Lady of Succour – an ironic day indeed for anyone to commit suicide. An overview of the dossier dominates the next plot bead. We are only on the third page of the script, but in the fifth plot bead of this extraordinarily densely woven little play. "A" then notices a bright star in the night sky, and this second astronomical eye-catcher neatly brackets the summary of the dossier's many rubrics.

Noticing the star (and discussing whether it is the planet Jupiter or the Dog Star, Sirius) marks the end of the first major *movement* of the play – a sequence that has all the formal characteristics of a prologue. By the end of this sequence, all the necessary elements of the play are assembled and identified (A, B, the Jumper C, his dossier, the date, our location, the issue). An unmistakable hinge-line leads us into the main body of the action:

B: Well? Do we work or play?

A systematic presentation of B's case, supporting the pre-emptive conclusion "Let him jump," follows in the next extended passage of the play. There are many individual parts to this section, as B reads excerpts from seven selected documents, but the sequential readings follow the formal procedures of a jury trial, or of a judicial inquiry. The segment ends in the re-iterated conclusion that this is an open and shut case:

A: We pack up this evening, right?
B: Without fail.

Then A has a last hunch to play. Was there not, under the rubric "Confidences," an extended piece of self-analysis (the sort of thing a therapist might have asked a depressed patient to prepare for a session)? B rummages, finds the documents, and begins a reading of this most personal and poignant of the documents when a very funny piece of comic stage business intervenes: B's desk lamp malfunctions and starts blinking erratically on and off, hilariously interrupting the painful first-person confessional writing. This counterpoint duet with the desk lamp is pure Beckett: a sardonic slap-stick routine at the exact point of maximum expressed pain and anguish. Content and form play in exaggerated interference patterns, to such a degree that in performance, the mechanical comedy almost completely masks the excruciating confession. This routine ends when B gives up in exasperation, utterly defeated by the faulty lamp.

B's distraught distress plays as a separate bead in the play, but the plot-bead diagram "holds open" the *shape* of the interrupted bead (the reading of the self-writing) because it is eventually resumed, finished, and it closes the main action of the play: "to sum up and clear out." While the action of the larger bead is temporarily suspended, however, "A" makes his second trip to the jumper's window, and it is a significant formal marker at the midpoint of the entire play. "A" brings with him on this excursus a poignant document from the dossier: a record of C's disturbing childhood truancies – a document he reads aloud while standing inches away from the miserable agonist. This visit (and the reading of the record) leads to a careful close-up scrutiny of C's face (presumably a search for the effect of A and B's review of his dossier) and at this formal "eye of the storm" there is a telltale stage direction:

Long pause, all three dead still.

Such an instruction is characteristic of a composer who is "listening to time," in Dante's phrase. It tends to occur in any script sculpted consciously out of deeply imagined rhythmic units – in other words, in masterful works composed for performance. Upon his return to his desk, A urges B to resume and complete the interrupted bead. When the reading is concluded, B emphatically rests his case as he violently slaps his hand on the pile of papers and declares:

B: There's the record, closed and final. That's what we're going on.

Now a formal summation commences (the promised "summing up") and the principal action of the play is coming to a clear-cut, well-orchestrated rhetorical ending, when a cat miaows unexpectedly. All interruptions are rhythmic plot markers (by definition), and the small cat motif, while it ominously delays (or announces?) the devastating conclusion ("Let him jump, let him jump"), also heightens the unmistakable "sense of an ending." In fact, the play's principal action ends here. A small break, or discontinuity in the plot-bead diagram indicates this "finished" form.

   Rough for Theatre II stands out among Beckett's stage plays because it has appended to it an extended coda. The play's strange tailpiece prolongs the playing past the clear formal end achieved by B's closing summation. After checking his watch and discovering (quite absurdly) that they have "no train before eleven twenty," A proposes a new plot bead that could stand as a definition of the typical theatrical "unit of duration":

A: Let us kill the time here, talking of this and that.

"Killing time" is a strange expression, and a disturbing one if dwelt upon too seriously. But the wonderfully whimsical and desultory theatrical *drifting* which Beckett composed to close *Rough for Theatre II* bears formal resemblances to the "Dead of Night" coda in *Julius Caesar* analyzed above. Purposeful *shape* to the dramatic structure simply ceases, as the action stops being "driven" by a clear-cut objective. We are in an "aftermath," the swirling, amorphous wake of a completed action.

The coda begins with a "hinge" of desultory conversation – and here the script resembles for a brief few lines Eugène Ionesco's classic send-up of desultory parlor conversation, *The Bald Soprano*. But the short hinge is suddenly given focus by the singing and fluttering of a bird in a hidden place onstage. A search for this bird, its discovery in a shrouded cage, and an inspection by match light of the contents of the cage (A and B discover a dead female in the cage with the singing male) constitute a whole "passage" in the play that the plot-bead diagram lumps together as the "Finches Business." This bird action eventually returns attention (for the last time) to the jumper, C – leading in turn to A's last trip to the window. The final small action (and bead) of the play is the discovery, in the light of a lit match, that C has begun to weep. The play-form closes on this tear drop.

Why is the coda there? What does it add to the play? What is the significance of the birds in the cage? Why are the two advocates allowed (by Beckett) to linger in the stage space after the play's principal action ("to sum up and clear out") is over? Does C jump or doesn't he?

The coda demands interpretation, and it is full of clues that converge on a "reading" of the thematic "content." But rhythmically, it imitates the flow of *unguided action*, the eerie formless twilight of "killing time," when characters stumble on from one involuntary discovery to the next, with random animal actions (the fluttering of the bird) and stray native curiosity (in the two advocates) the only apparent forces pulling the time-form along. Note how *different* this is from the usual *willed* scene in a drama. It is similar, however, to Shakespeare's coda, and the *drift* of Brutus alone in his tent preparing for bed, unable to sleep, disquiet, preoccupied, erratically shifting from improvised moment to improvised moment.

In the Shakespeare, a ghost invades the coda. I think an analogous "spirit" enters Beckett's play during the coda, but readers and audience members can disagree with this interpretation. My hunch is that the missing "Lady of Succour," whose day this is, operates in the closing moments through the volitional voids of the coda. The jumper seems to be moved by the clumsily revealed *figura* of the birds (one dead, one left living) to feel pity outside himself, and, perhaps, to glimpse an obligation *to go on*. If this is correct, the coda provides an intercession beyond the competence of the farcical paracletes, A and B, whose crude review of C's dossier reached only the callous conclusion "Let him jump." We watch in the coda a mystery of seemingly random operation, as the jumper's heart is (perhaps) softened and re-directed. In this reading, C might well *not* jump. But Beckett's finished form makes neither outcome certain.

To play the music of Beckett's form we do not need to insist on a definitive answer to either question. We need, as performers, only to achieve the scripted end with great delicacy and rhythmic fidelity to the suggestion of pity (and hope?) that closes the form. No "content" analysis can get us there. Our only "score" for this is the rhythmic form.

Aristotle's proposition in *The Poetics*: linking *Form* to *Action*

In the short, semi-chaotic bundle of notes that has survived from antiquity as *The Poetics*, Aristotle carefully (and I think accurately) delimited what "dramatic form" consisted of in the examples familiar to him. This chapter has been discussing the continued relevance and wide application of Aristotle's insight into dramatic form. But Aristotle also ventured a bold proposition that goes beyond his formal definitions. He flatly declared that human action (*praxis*) is the generating principle behind dramatic form. Put another way, he suggested that action is prior (both *logically* and *temporally*) to our animal motions in response to *action*. These reactive *motions* (or what we might call *enactments* of the motive impulse) include the words characters utter, which are frequently the most misleading elements in a script. The *words* in a script are misleading because they make action claims, but they mask the action as frequently as they reveal it. Action is what forms the *need to speak*, and a definite action must therefore be already in progress *before* a character utters words. Whenever we spontaneously speak, we do so because we are already animated by a mental focus and objective that has *an instrumental need* for language. That *need-prior-to-speech* reflects our action at that moment of speaking. The actual words that issue from our mouths may (and usually do) have any old haphazard relation to the underlying action, depending on our verbal skill, our self-consciousness, our so-called *articulateness*, our clarity of mind, and many other factors. In a drama, the underlying *action* is all that matters.

"Action" is, furthermore, the clarifying term for those (numerous in the profession) who confuse story with plot. For story/plot interactions cannot be grasped or "solved" (when there is a problem with either the plot or the story) without grasping the underlying action that is in progress (or trying to come into being, into performance) in the script. Aristotle thus bequeathed to us a proposition that still holds center stage in drama theory: the proposition that theatrical form *imitates* an action. He linked *action* and *form* in a way that was compelling, given the example of the theatre of fifth-century Athens. Aristotle deduced his observation (which later generations tried to make into a rule) from available examples of the drama in his time. There is much to learn that is practical and eminently useful in *The Poetics*, as we shall see by taking Aristotle's proposition seriously: if the *form* of a play (the arrangement of the incidents) "imitates an action," then what, exactly *is* an action? Can we understand *action* in such a way that Aristotle's proposition holds? In the next chapter, we will carefully review this second principle of dramaturgy, and explore what it might mean for the time-form (the plot) to be so crafted as to be the principal means by which an action (praxis) is imitated in a play.

References

Beckett, S. (1976) *Rough for Theatre II* in *Ends and Odds*. New York: Grove Press.

Butcher, S.H. and Aristotle (1951) *Aristotle's Poetics*. Translated 1895, Introduction by H. Gassner. New York: Dover Publications, Inc.

Butcher, S.H. and Aristotle (1961) *Aristotle's Poetics*. Translated 1895, Introduction by F. Fergusson. New York: Hill and Wang.

Lessing, G. (1984) *Laocoön*. Translated by E.A. McCormick, 1962 for Bobbs-Merrill Company. Baltimore: Johns Hopkins University Press. (Originally published 1766.)

Michelangelo Buonarroti (1991) The Poetry of Michelangelo. Translated by J.M. Saslow. New Haven: Yale University Press

Pine-Coffin, R.S. and Saint Augustine (1961) *Confessions*. Baltimore: Penguin Classics.

Sheed, F.J. and Saint Augustine (1943) *Confessions of St. Augustine*. New York: Sheed and Ward.

Shyer, L. (1989) *Robert Wilson and His Collaborators*. New York: TCG.

Stanislavski, K. (1980) *An Actor Prepares*. Translated by E.R. Hapgood, 1937. London: Methuen. (Originally published 1936.)

2 Action

Action as a term of art

No single term in the theatre is more central or more widely underestimated and misapplied than is the term *action*. Part of the problem with the word, as I mentioned in the Introduction, is that it is a common one in English, with widespread colloquial usage, and one that most speakers of the language do not see as particularly difficult or obscure in its meaning. Everyone has a fairly secure sense that they know what the word *action* means, without needing any special instruction in overtones of significance. But *action* happens also to be the only sensible English equivalent for Aristotle's *praxis* – his most important term of definition in *The Poetics*, and as such, it acquires a special status as a "term of art." The principle of dramaturgy I mean to discuss in this chapter is best called *action*, but we must be prepared to take it in its second, fully technical sense in what follows, and not let the easy colloquial understanding of it confuse a deep artisanal need to get the concept right (for practical purposes) and to stick to its context of application in creative theatre work.

The American scholars Francis Fergusson and Kenneth Burke studied Aristotle with care, extracting from his ancient thought insights highly pertinent to contemporary dramaturgy and to the modern analysis of action. Fergusson, for his part, was also among the first Americans to receive in-depth training in Stanislavski technique, for he became in 1925 the Associate Director of the American Laboratory Theatre in New York, where Richard Boleslavsky and Maria Ouspenskaya introduced Stanislavski's System to a very influential generation of American actors and directors. Trained as he was in philosophy before he went into the theatre, Fergusson was the first in the United States to note the correlation between Stanislavski's seat-of-the-pants (first-hand) pragmatic intuitions about dramatic action and Aristotle's 2400-year-old observations about the importance of *praxis*. Discerning unbroken patterns of *mimesis praxeos* – or "imitation of action" – in *all* dramaturgy, whether ancient or modern, Fergusson revived our understanding of *action* as an aesthetic term by referring it to Aristotle's *Poetics*:

> The word "action" – praxis – as Aristotle uses it in The Poetics, does not mean outward deeds or events, but something more like "purpose" or "aim." Perhaps our word "motive" suggests most of its meaning. Dante (who in this respect is a sophisticated Aristotelian) uses the phrase moto spiritale – spiritual movement – to indicate praxis. In Aristotle's own writings praxis is usually rational, a movement of the will in the light of the mind. But Dante's moto spiritale refers to all modes of the spirit's life, all of its directions, or focuses, or motives, including those of childhood, dream, drunkenness or passion, which are hardly rationalized at all. When using Aristotle's definition for the analysis of modern drama it is necessary to generalize his notion of action in this way, to include movements of the spirit in response to sensuous or emotionally charged images as well as consciously willed purpose. But this seems to me a legitimate extension of the basic concept; and I do not think it does violence to Aristotle's meaning.
>
> (Fergusson, 1957, p. 115)

Whether or not Fergusson does violence to Aristotle's notion of *praxis* in the above extension of its meaning (classicists and philosophers who specialize in Aristotle concede that Aristotle meant different things by *praxis* in different contexts), he makes available to contemporary artists a valuable aesthetic tool with immediate practical utility. Action understood as the life of human consciousness itself – its capacity to experience the world, to will its own responses to it, and to suffer the buffets of fate and circumstance – is indeed the basic subject matter of all the arts, ancient, medieval, and modern. Dante's extension of what Aristotle may have meant by *praxis* is still derived (by way of Thomas Aquinas) from Aristotelian tenets. Thus, Fergusson's deeply historical "reading" of *The Poetics* – a text that is drastically abbreviated, abrupt and cursory in the fragmentary fourth century B.C. form in which it has survived – persuasively restores its vitality and applicability as a poetics.

In *The Poetics* Aristotle famously defines a tragedy as – and I quote S.H. Butcher's translation of the Greek – "an imitation of an action (*mimesis praxeos*) that is serious, complete, and of a certain magnitude" (Butcher and Aristotle, 1951, p. 23). W. Hamilton Fyfe, another translator and commentator of *The Poetics*, points out that the meaning of *praxis* in Aristotle's usage "includes what the hero does and what happens to him" (Fyfe and Aristotle, 1932, p. 22). He links this meaning to another passage, in Chapter 2 of *The Poetics* (ibid., p. 9), where Aristotle states that "men doing or experiencing something" are the *objects* of mimetic representation – and this squares easily with our common experience of what a play on the stage consists of. It is the primary job of the plot (*mythos*) – defined as "the arrangement of the incidents" – to imitate the action (*praxis*) of the play.

The idea that "an action that is serious, complete, and of a certain magnitude" is the basic principle by which a play achieves aesthetic unity and distinctive stature as a work of art happens to coincide with one of the twentieth-century's greatest philosophical forays into aesthetics: John Dewey's *Art as Experience* (1934). Dewey used the term "experience" rather than *action* (with stress on the special conditions that produce what we call "*an* experience") where Aristotle used *praxis* – but we can readily see that Dewey chose "experience" over "action" in English precisely because it includes what commentators tell us *praxis* included in Greek: *that which a person experiences* as well *that which a person does*. (Dewey's exact phrase (1934, p. 264) is "things done and things undergone.") Such usage correlates as well (and far from accidentally) with Stanislavski's formulation that it is the drama's task to track "the life of the human psyche" with meticulous attention and fidelity. In a very influential article first published in *Theatre Workshop* in 1936, the Russian director I.M. Rapoport stated Stanislavski's position starkly:

> Action is not only external, i.e., connected with motion in the course of which man changes his position in space, but also internal (psychological) taking place in the consciousness of man and causing a change of his mental condition.
>
> (Cole and Rapoport, 1995, p. 60)

Our knowledge and use of *action* in contemporary theatre practice owes a great debt to Stanislavski (and I will review that legacy below), but another powerful guide to action-lore – one whose writings can also help us grasp quickly and surely what the concept means – is Kenneth Burke. Burke (who died in 1993 at the age of 96) was a thinker hard to classify; he eluded pigeonholing all his life. Literary critics claimed him as one of their own; sociologists were, for a time (and may even remain), his most devoted fans and followers. I think he can be very useful to students of the theatre, especially on the topic of *action*.

Kenneth Burke's lifelong pursuit of a "grammar of motives" led him to formulate a system he rather awkwardly called "Dramatism" by which he strove to systematize discourse and analysis of every variety of human action. "What is involved, when we say what people are doing and why they are doing it?" he asked at the outset of his huge compendium of Dramatism, *A Grammar of Motives* (Burke, 1969, p. xv). He offers as his answer a "pentad of dramatistic terms" – rubrics by which he seeks to contain and determine the essentials of *any* action by circumscribing them with five key terms: Act, Scene, Agent, Agency, and Purpose. Burke's pentad is a useful schematic by which to deepen one's familiarity with *action* as a term of art. We can readily see the pentad's relevance to the drama when we see what the five terms seek to answer: what was it that was done? (Act); where and when was it done? (Scene); who did it? (Agent); how was it done? (Agency); and why? (Purpose). These are all obvious dramaturgical questions anyone needs to ask and answer when approaching a script. And his analysis of "ratios" between the terms – by which he means how *scene* might condition *act*, or *agent* condition *purpose*, etc. – offers very fertile methods for dramaturgical exploration, which I will treat at greater length in Chapter 3, where Production Dramaturgy will be our topic. Burke's is admittedly a dryer, "after-the-fact," forensic approach to action that lacks the organic dynamism of the Fergussonian–Aristotelian approach, but it is not hard to see that under the guise of "dramatism" it treats the same subject as the drama. Burke's pentad orients the mind swiftly to the *nature* of what is being sought at the core of dramatic art works.

Philosophers throughout the two-and-a-half millennia since Aristotle have struggled to formulate satisfactory technical definitions of human *action*, and the ancient tradition of discourse and speculation on *action* (at first directed almost exclusively toward ethics and moral rectitude, and later to their extensions in politics, civil and criminal law, and ecclesiastical rules and regulations) has been augmented in the last century by psychoanalytic insights and theories, by the observational science of behaviorism, by the relatively new disciplines of sociology and anthropology and, most recently, by the astounding advances of the cognitive sciences – advances which in themselves have triggered a revolution in philosophical "models" for human cognition, volition, and the "life" of the mind.

In the theatre *action* is quite simply our most important "term of art" – and no one engaged professionally in the field should ever be vague or fuzzy-minded about it. We need to know what an *action* is, what one looks like, feels like, and sounds like. We need to be able to know one when we see one, or – equally importantly – to tell immediately when one is missing, or when a theatrical scene is trying to "go" with a feeble or insufficient action, or when a scene is being rehearsed with the wrong assumed action. Nine times out of ten, a "dead" scene in a new script is bandying words about with no clear underlying action at all.

We need not entirely abandon the colloquial, or common-sense meaning of *action*, to grasp the technical, artisanal meaning of the term (as a principle of dramaturgy). The term of art *contains* the usual meaning of "action" in English. But we must be prepared, as Fergusson suggested, to extend that meaning and to study the thing we mean by *action* closely until its deeper nature becomes second nature and we can *think* of one at will.

Complete actions

Let's start with the character's action within the play, for seizing this fictional action is the logical first step in figuring out what the *actor* (and everyone else in the theatre) is supposed to be doing. What is *an action*, and why should the topic be difficult and elusive? Don't we all – whether we are in the theatre or not – know perfectly well what an action is? Newspaper headlines are full of obvious actions, are they not? "Britons vote to leave the European Union!"; "Father kidnaps infant daughters from estranged wife"; "Murder suspect kills two detectives and a state trooper, then shoots self." "President denies he colluded with Russians." The verb in these headlines tells us the action: vote, kidnaps, kills, denies. So far, the topic of action is not problematic. But if we start thinking of re-enactment of such actions, or portrayal via performance – i.e., if we start thinking theatrically – these actions and their shorthand notation in language grow densely complex. How would you dramatize the campaign and the vote in the U.K., or an angry divorcé kidnapping two baby girls, or the whole sorry debacle of multiple murders, manhunt, and suicide, or the formal public act of refuting an accusation – one move in a tangled series of political strategies and "damage control"? These things we try to call "actions" are invariably the end terms of a complex story, the culminating point of a long series of circumstances woven out of prior actions, prior circumstances. Television thrusts "headline" images of such culminating actions relentlessly at us, intensifying our consciousness that "something happened" (this consciousness is what we call "news") but baffling any understanding of what these actions mean. The typical television "dramatization" of such actions thrusts an obvious, usually violent, or titillating image of the *event* at us, but such images are little more than crude stagings of what passes through the average imagination on simply hearing of the news: this thing happened. If anything, the vivid apparent Realism of television images, even when they record the actual events as they take place, heighten our realization that we barely know "what is going on." The headlines in the paper and online are "grabbers" or "clickbait" designed to make us read on for more information, for a deeper grasp of the underlying *action* hinted at by the external deed. Any serious theatricalization of an action is a re-exploration (usually but not always with the intent of being *explanatory*) of what it was that happened. This is what Aristotle was harping on when he insisted, in *The Poetics*, that a good play is the imitation of a *complete* action. The Aristotelian insistence on completeness, on a sort of holistic comprehensiveness is evidently directed at such an expansion of the superficial constatation of a mere event, and in this observation, Aristotle was summing up the wisdom behind all good storytelling. In a play, we want to know "the whole story."

The expansion of an event into a narrative is an age-old cultural device for deploying the *wholeness* of an action before our attentive minds. Most good stories capitalize on the contrast between the decisive event, or the *crisis* in the action – the fragment of the whole that is traditionally used as a shorthand for the whole (the thing we seldom miss, because it makes itself felt as memorable news) – and the "whole story" of which that fragment is the culmination. Actions, according to Aristotle, are large organic structures, with beginnings, middles, and ends. And when actions are comprehended fully by an observant mind, they can then be imitated by performance and by the analogy of a plot structure. Plots cannot be built except as sequences of incidents, and the form of such plots, Aristotle suggests, will be *analogous* to the full natural history of a complete action. The basic dramaturgy of crime drama follows the five forensic terms of Burke's pentad: what happened, when and where, who did it, how, and why? We may see a crude, violent, shocking image of The Event as a prelude to the story, and then a "flashback" sequence that lays the ground for *how* it happened, then follows step by step as a witches' brew of character, circumstance, passion and desire, rage and accident leads fatefully back to the decisive moment that made the *action* news. Such construction is elementary dramaturgy: the re-creation of events arranged such that we see, step by step, *how* some known event happened. So what do we properly call "The Action" in all this? The whole structure is properly imitating "The Action," and it differs from the news bulletin or the newspaper headline in that it is now made, or attempted to be made, complete.

Action is the whole complex within a human being that "moves" that human being to bestir him- or herself in the world, to undertake something, to manifest the living presence of a Self. Thus *action* is both internal and external; it is a mysterious private amalgam of obscure "movements" within the psyche, and it is also overt, visible physical moves outside in the light of day. In the theatre, we re-enact the physical and visible moves *in order to* reveal and portray the otherwise hidden and invisible inner life of the psyche, where the existence of the Self "takes place." We feature the external act to reveal the internal action. Such statements are attempts to define an action, and they make use of spatial metaphors (movement, inside, outside) to get a grip on the nature of an action. They are attempts to "get the whole picture." These metaphors are in their own right an involuntary *theory* of the drama, and this makes it more than plausible that there is something completely circular going on in our theoretical language about the theatre. Everything points to the idea that the theatre was invented and practiced – *in the first place* – to do just what the struggle *to define* an action recapitulates: to reveal the hidden springs of human action – another spatial metaphor. Aristotle was the first to define theatrical art as fixed and centered on human action, and the subsequent history of the theatre has tended to prove his formulation of principle essentially right: *action* seemingly inevitably resurfaces – in every style, in every age – as the gravitational core of everything we do in the theatre.

Aristotle's notion of a complete action

Francis Fergusson, as quoted above, was highly circumspect in extending the meaning of *praxis* to include Dante's larger *moto spiritale*, thus covering any and all "movements" of the psyche (and converging with the teaching of Stanislavski). But Aristotle is on record as proposing, in writings other than *The Poetics*, a sort of natural history of a complete action as he concluded it must necessarily unfold within an individual human agent. In his *Peri Psyches* (the *De Anima*) – a text infrequently studied by theatre people – Aristotle placed in a sort of "natural progression" a *causal* sequence that is, in effect, a slow-motion, exploded study of what *must take place* when conscious human beings undertake to do things. His resulting analysis can be laid out schematically as an *anatomy of an action*, and though such a painstaking analytical study presents an *action* in a highly unnatural way (it is "unnatural" in exactly the same sense that a dissected corpse is no longer "natural" after an autopsy) the dissected action can very usefully be studied and pondered if one's objective is to acquire a reliable practical reflex for *discerning* action. After contemplating analytical models, the artist can transport acquired insights back to the natural, "live" contexts of real actions, and apply any deepened insight to the organic business of re-presenting actions. In any case, the term *praxis*, left undefined and in need of extension in *The Poetics*, does have an Aristotelian elaboration that helps us grasp the intended meaning of his definition of a tragedy in Chapter VI of his *Poetics*. The following schematized anatomy of a complete Aristotelian action is derived principally from the *Peri Psyches* (*On the Soul*, Hett and Aristotle, 1957), but it is buttressed by ideas found in Aristotle's *Nicomachean Ethics* and in his *Politics*. It can still help cement an *image* of what a "complete action" was meant to mean, and that image is still usefully implanted in the mind of a contemporary drama student.

Anatomy of an action

1 An action has its deepest origins in perception (*aesthesis*), or the functioning of the five senses. Through these familiar senses (sight, hearing, touch, taste, smell), the inner psyche "drinks in" impressions of the external World. These are the front lines of the Self's interaction with the World. Sensation is *logically prior* to any subsequent action of the self in the world.

2 Mental activity (*dianoia*) then pools sense-data in what Aristotle called the "common sense" (*term in Greek: κοινον αισθητηριον*). This *sensus communis*, as it was translated in Latin versions of Aristotle, corresponds exactly to what contemporary cognitive science struggles to define as the notorious "binding problem": how are sense-data made into holistic images in the mind, and what physiological mechanism creates unitary experience out of the welter of bio-mechanical stimuli which feed into the brain? All we know for sure is that it happens.

3 There follows, in Aristotelian analysis, a determination of a "Good" (or the notorious "perceived good" of the philosophers), which is the outcome of *dianoia*, mental activity operating on what it thinks it perceives. Every "object" seen in the world, Aristotle suggested, strikes the perceiver as good, bad, or indifferent.

4 Desire (*orexis*), follows. This is the psychological "engine" of attraction or aversion. *Orexis* usually defines a goal (*telos*) for there is no expression of desire without an object: one desires *something*. Any object can be perceived without being desired, but *orexis* fuses with its object in the moment of desiring: and once formed, desire can subsist without the physical presence of its object. The motive force of most plays is contained in this one observation. This step in a complete action is usually experienced as "fated" by most human beings, as something that acts within them independently of their conscious will. We seem to be "visited" by appetite and desires, and the more violent they are, the better they are suited for the drama. Note too, that this mechanism can and does operate as attraction and pursuit (toward a good) or revulsion and flight (from a bad). "Love" and "hate" are not irrelevant terms here.

5 Practical reasoning (*bouleusis*) follows, in some but not all cases, the identification of an object of desire. Aristotle called the virtue of consistent good deliberation about one's actions *phronesis*. Such an internal process within the psyche is of particular interest for the drama, and scenes of *bouleusis* are frequently portrayed in the theatre. In such scenes, we witness (usually very artificially) the formulation of a plan

of action, or the deliberate devising of practical means to an envisioned end. This is a staple resource of conventional dramaturgy. Think of lovers devising ways to approach their beloved, or bastards planning how they can harm their enemies. The characters within the play are planning the plot of the play in such scenes – one reason why this highly artificial dramaturgical device is so popular among playwrights.

6 Next, for things to keep going, there has to be a will to act. Actors frequently call this "impulse." Aristotle called it *horme*, but scholars caution against equating anything in Aristotle with the complex struggles of *willing* found much later, for instance, in the writings of Augustine, who explored the murky territory of one's inability to act on a conscious desire. In any case, some applied energy transforms *potentiality* into *actuality*, capacity into act, plan into "action," in the colloquial usage. Aristotle called that transformation, *energeia*. Some people can generate this impulse directly out of desire, others need to be provoked into impulse by an external agency, and still others fail to act on desire or impulse (the notorious "Hamlet Effect"). All variations of the will to act are endlessly explored in the drama – so much so that many people unwittingly identify "drama" and "the dramatic" with the strong emotions frequently associated with the triggering impulse of will. Emotions are not, however, the constitutive element of any action. Many of the most hackneyed and familiar devices of dramaturgy have to do with this tipping point into the next stage in our anatomy.

7 THE ACT ITSELF. This is the point of no return, the crisis, the climax and the turning point of a complete action. (Technically, the turning point is often delayed in a play, usually so it can be studied at more leisure in the artistic form.) This step alone – "the flagrant act" – is often misleadingly abstracted into the whole meaning of the word "action." That limited colloquial usage of the word *action* is one of the greatest obstacles to a deeper, more sophisticated understanding of the term. *Action* becomes our most valuable "term of art" when it means a whole, complex organic process worked out to completion. This exact moment of the anatomy is the best moment to ponder the difference between the loose everyday meaning we might give to *action* and the richer, more complex technical meaning that becomes such a powerful tool for serious theatre artists. Few plays omit *staging* step 7, so it is seen "live" before the audience. But the few plays that do omit "the Act Itself" prove just how detachable it is from the "complete action" that is our real object of interest.

8 The act leads invariably to "The Suffering of its Consequences" (*pathos*); *someone* always suffers the brunt of every action-in-the-world. (Existentialism focuses great attention on this inevitable

linkage between steps 7 and 8); pain and suffering, blood and guts, casualty-littered battlefields, go here. Also inner anguish, pain, grief, or elation. Tragedies almost invariably linger unnaturally in their portrayal of these pathetic emotions. The reason is that they fascinate and appall us in real life: we stand transfixed at the spectacle of immediate suffering, perhaps because we see in it the one thing we most fear – and can least control – in life.

Another way to image the watershed of step 7 is to consider that in steps 1 through 6, the external World has been impinging on the inner Self of the protagonist. Starting with step 7, *The Act*, the Self asserts itself on the world, and counter-acts on it. The period during which people "suffer the consequences of an act" is really a period of complex disequilibrium in the world brought about by specific human agency. It pinpoints (usually) our highest interest in the subject of action. Structurally, it is frequently here that we find "the point" and the payoff of a good play.

9 The detailed anatomy continues with a Renewed Perception (*mathema*) after suffering. This can also be described as the mind's evaluation of the "success" or "failure" of its original end, or "*telos.*" "It is the final end that is the initial cause in conduct," Aristotle tells us in the *De Anima* (Hammond and Aristotle, 1902, p. 132). That desired goal has either been reached or missed by the act. Or the act reveals by its consequences that the "perceived Good" was formulated erroneously. Everyone can sense by the very description of such an outcome that tragedy is lurking in the wings here. Tragic suffering will very obviously be triggered by the perception at this stage – i.e., too late – of an error. Comic revel will, conversely, be unleashed by the happy achievement of a goal that proves accurate and as good as it seemed at the outset. This ninth phase is accurately described as "learning from experience." It is also usually portrayed in that portion of a play that is clearly the "wind-down," or the beginning of the end. It is worth musing on this all-too-obvious correlation between a descriptive sequence meant to define "a complete action" and the *form* of plays we already know from experience. We are getting ready to understand Aristotle's ensuing proposition: that the *form* of a play (the arrangement of its incidents) *imitates* a complete action.

10 Finally, an Illumination (epiphany) closes the sequence. The Greek plays studied by Aristotle always had a formal coda where the expression of some new knowledge was presented as a finale. These final steps (after step 7) represent the famous "pathemathos" of Aeschylus, or the law – attributed to Zeus himself – of "suffering into truth." It is typical of Aristotle's philosophical predilections that an action would

not be considered complete or significant until it had yielded some increment of knowledge. But subsequent theatre practice has repeatedly confirmed this predilection.

These closing sequences are the learning phase "sinking in" and creating new *character* in front of our eyes, *transforming* character. We like to call this "character growth," which reassures us by suggesting that "suffering is not in vain." Without some sort of extracted "lesson" from suffering, most audiences have felt robbed of a proper sense of an ending.

Such an exploded view of a "complete action" is as stated above, artificial. Real people in real situations do not proceed so methodically and "by the book" as this analysis implies. Nor are the ten steps above ever presented by Aristotle or anyone else as a literal plan for the writing of a play. But the meticulous artificiality of the analysis is deeply analogous to the difference between a real "action-in-the-world" and an artistic imitation of an action in a play. The imitation in a play is re-conceptualized at a higher level of human awareness, one that is intrinsically more rational, more knowing, and better understood than the original action as it may have occurred in nature (or in "real life"). Such a re-conceptualization of an action is the work of a dramatic poet, and actors must learn to match their instincts and mimetic skills to the knowledge and information already captured formally in a finished script. This view of the playwright's art (*poiesis*) as a more philosophical re-presentation of real life is essentially the Aristotelian "mimetic" theory of the drama. In whatever way we may wish to modify these observations, they form a still-useful starting point for formulating a practical theory by which to practice dramatic art.

Practical handles for grasping "an action"

At any one moment of time or experience, one's consciousness should be able to take the pulse of the ongoing action. As long as we are alive, an action is in progress – but what is it in each particular instance? We find it by noticing *where the psyche is focused*, what is holding its full attention, how the seat of consciousness is engaged. Our eyes are extremely sensitive to our actions, and almost invariably are focused on some important external correlative to our action (and eye focus is perhaps the most important single indicator in performance). But our whole bodies can also "focus" on our action, and just as completely. It is the *psyche*, the seat of consciousness (sometimes thought of as the Self) that determines the action. The tests we apply in real life are the same we apply in trying to figure out the action in a theatrical scene, or the action in a poem (a tricky thing to discern), or the action in a real-life interaction in a grocery store, or the action hidden in the formal arcana of a legal document or a "financial instrument." If we develop a good enough "feel" for what an ongoing action is, we can set about observing and studying actions everywhere; the subject becomes accessible, and it becomes possible to talk of the *action* of a passage of music, or the *action* of a painting or the *action* of a sculpture. Anything manmade has built into it an action "print," like a fingerprint. We leave highly conscious and intentional action-prints of this kind on everything we humans come in contact with. Some philosophers have gone so far as to speculate whether *causation* (one of the great tenets of western science) might be nothing but an *unwarranted analogy* to what humans experience as their own truculent agency in the world: we "see" ourselves messing about with everything we can see and reach – is not some analogous agency "causing" all the motion and change we witness in the world? Our "action" – we know this because we do it – pushes the objects of the world around at our will. We are convinced we know this "from experience." Conversely (so we reason) when we experience the world, in its turn, knocking *us* around (sunburns, limbs falling from trees, rockslides, rainstorms, floods, hurricanes, earthquakes) and "messing with our heads" (i.e., causing moods, fears, dreams, visions, voices), we cannot help but ask (from our "experience" of things) what agency is "doing" these things? The drama has been a major means of asking such questions and probing for answers.

Good actors, in every age, have always been valued for their "gut feel" for actions.

What we mean by that "feel" is a knack for access to the triggers in human personality that unleash a *need* to do something. In the theatre, that "something" is whatever the script indicates gets done (including, but not limited to, what dialogue is spoken). The key talent, however, if one is concerned with the art of the drama, is the instinct to seek and find something *prior* to (and far more important than) the mere "thing done"; the key histrionic instinct works like a reflex in gifted theatre artists: it almost automatically unearths any specified action's probable *motive*, or its triggering impulse in the human psyche. Ironically, one of the worst clues to the core of an action is often what a character *says* while engaged in that action: for speech is the great masker, the great rational dissimulator; we speak more often to *conceal* our action (from others and from ourselves) than to reveal it. Good plays are written by dramatists who know the ironic function of speech, and great actors always sense their way below the misleading surface of words. Rare is the character (in a *good* play) who speaks clear thoughts that are accurate expressions of their core actions. (Shakespeare's young women are notable examples of an exception to this general rule.) Stanislavski and his disciples formulated the idea of "subtext" to contrast the apparent content of speech to underlying *action*.

Good actors frequently report that they "feel" the nascent contours of an action in the pit of their stomachs, or deeper in the gut, in what T'ai Chi adepts identify as the central locus of the *qi* life force. Aristotle, in the treatise *Peri Psyches* from which much of the above anatomy is drawn, indicated a similar seat of impulsion that he located in the chest, closer to the solar plexus. I have found my own best "feel" as a director trying (in sympathy with my actors) to scope the dynamic of a scene, to come from that place from which I had been trained to move when I was a competitive collegiate wrestler, some place near the internal muscles that control my center of gravity – I suspect it may be the same cluster of deep central muscles identified with the flow of the "qi." Dancers tell me it correlates to that place in the body where the criss-crossing internal muscles in the pelvis link the upper body to the lower body, producing (and controlling) the motions of both. Dancers learn to "lift" from that center, as though they were consciously grasping their own spine at its base, and carrying it like a hoisted flagpole. These examples are all attempts to assign a conscious physical location to a "place" that can just as well be metaphorical: it is the inner "place" from which the Self "springs into action."

Stanislavski's legacy

Stanislavski's influence in the American theatre has dominated the twentieth century, but the authority of his "System" – or more accurately, the American "Method" evolved by Stanislavski's many disciples – has by now grown old. But the *action* baby should not be thrown out with the psycho-babble bathwater of one peculiarly "psycho-intensive" training technique. The *action* in each scene of a play (whether the style is Realism or not) still needs to be known, and the word "motivation" is not an irrelevant guide to that action. Some good acting teachers (like Richard Hornby in *The End of Acting* (2000)) have preferred to have students identify action *objectives* rather than wallow in *motivations* for actions, but Hornby substitutes this more neutral, more objective vocabulary mainly to break the Strasbergian psycho-cycle and to get actors out of their own heads and back to the task of *acting* parts from scripts. *Praxis-action* as a permanent principle of dramaturgy, however, is not affected by the shift in actor emphasis represented by avoiding *motivation* and substituting *objective* in the working vocabulary of the rehearsal hall.

The concept of *action* deserves to be freed from any *exclusive* association with "inner" technique, or with the so-called "psychological Realism" that has dogged Stanislavski-based work throughout the decades of his influence. These associations, which are understandable enough given the *applications* of the Method that prevailed in the 1930s and 1940s, misleadingly associate the theatrical styles of Realism or Naturalism (and with them plays that strive to express "social consciousness") with action analysis. Eugene Vakhtangov (who died in 1922) was the first of Stanislavski's disciples to demonstrate that there is no essential link between Stanislavski technique and any particular style or subject matter in the theatre. Vsevolod Meyerhold also made that clear in the early years of the twentieth century – well before the Stanislavski System was introduced to Americans, and Stanislavski himself was practicing his craft in openly "theatrical" (or *presentational*) styles by the time Depression-era Americans started invoking his name and authority. Stanislavski enthusiasts of the 1930s were really struggling to create American imitations of the "socially conscious" Modernist masterpieces of an already bygone era: the turn-of-the-century works of Maxim Gorki and Anton Chekhov.

In all cases of adapting Stanislavski's methodology in American theatre, the stress was on *actor training*. The larger dramaturgical consequences of a fully developed action-lore were always secondary in American theatre culture. In his work as a *director*, Stanislavski extended and generalized his notion of action with a powerful intuition of its *structural* (or *formal*) importance, thus reaching beyond the function he stressed while thinking and writing about actors and their *individual* skills. Directors were enjoined by Stanislavski to find the "action spine" of a play, or the "through-line" – sometimes also translated as the "transparent effect" of a script, or its "superobjective," which Stanislavski also freely equated with the *action* of the play. These deeper formal terms differ in important ways from an actor's consciousness of *his* or *her* action in individual scenes. Method actors were, to be sure, asked to discern their individual character's "arc of action" within a play, and they were further trained to sub-divide their individual trajectories into "action beats," but these still-useful practices do not automatically lead to full dramaturgical awareness of the *form* of a play.

This shift of focus from the individual psychology of action (actors' perspective on their *roles*) to the function of *the action* in the scene-by-scene architecture of plays (playwrights' and directors' perspective on *plots*) is a crucial one in dramaturgy. An individual character's action *in* a scene is not the same entity as the defining action *of* the scene. Action-lore for actors thus differs from action-lore for playwrights and directors, even though *action* continues to be the unifying term. The two senses of *action* differ primarily in a shift of attention from the private "inner" springs of *action* to the larger formal patterns of a plot (arrangement of the incidents). Another way to put the distinction is that directors are entrusted with the *formal cause* of a play (the subject of Chapter 1) while actors are simultaneously the chief *material cause* and the principal *efficient cause* of plays in performance.

If action is a cornerstone of all dramaturgy, it is so regardless of the *style* of that dramaturgy: nothing performed in any theatrical setting can ever escape the condition of being *an action*, in the purely technical sense. Stanislavski, in a famous training exercise he described in *An Actor Prepares* (1980), asked a student actor (a young woman) to sit still on the stage, alone and in silence in front of her watching classmates, during a brief but scrutinized interval between the opening and closing of the curtain. Stanislavski was brutal in criticizing her fidgeting, glancing about, and tugging at her skirt. He was trying to demonstrate that: *an actor of distinction should be able to sit without a motion and at the same time be centered in a calm interior action.* This is an important lesson about action and an actor's willed focus onstage: the artisanal sense of *action* is far more a question of interior being than of outward show. But there is another and equally important "lesson" which could have been learned from Stanislavski's example: the sitter in this exercise was *also* performing an action, and performing it perfectly, though it was one Stanislavski deemed a failure. She was striving to escape the humiliation she felt at being deliberately exposed to the gaze of her classmates. If a script called for her to perform that action, her performance would have been judged masterful.

I once witnessed a performance by Robert Wilson in which he took 30 minutes to cross from the wings stage right across the stage, accompanied the whole time by the recorded sound of massed harmonic chords from a brass choir. His motion was so slow it appeared static at any one glance, but it became clear he was never still, and that he was – almost miraculously – in constant uninterrupted "slow motion" making his way toward an objective I took (for the first 15 minutes) to be the center of the stage. When he did not stop there, but moved on past the midpoint – still at his excruciatingly slow but fluent and continuous pace – the audience giggled at the recognition of the apparent "form" of his movement. His dramaturgy could not have been more minimalist, or more legible. No matter what we do on a stage, that "doing" is legible; and it is legible because it correlates to an *inevitable* action in progress. When what we hope we are doing is acting a given part in a play (and acting the part well), the "inevitable" action we set in motion just by being there had better be the action we intend for the play. This is how art differs from "life." Stanislavski devised methods both for doing what we intend onstage (physical training, concentration, relaxation) and he developed methods for intending to do the right thing when assigned any particular role to play (action analysis of one's part in a play). These are still the two primary thrusts in all acting training today.

Action of the author

One major source of dramaturgical confusion (and theatrical malpractice) stems from the action of the author in composing a play. This action (*poiesis* in Aristotle's terminology) needs to be carefully and clearly differentiated from the "fictional" action of the characters represented in the play. If we take seriously the proposition that "all action is legible," then one can read and interpret the action of a composer of plays and scenes as well as the actions of the characters *within* the scenes. Such "reading" of motives in authors is a fertile field of *literary* criticism, especially in the postmodern era. When an author writes a "scene," he is in essence "staging" a mini-play for the imagination of his readers. Literary criticism is constantly engaged in upending inept attempts to pass off a *represented* action while an unexamined (or unsuspected) ulterior action is being involuntarily revealed. The fertile field of cultural criticism deconstructs, in this way, deeply encoded sociological attitudes and unexamined premises involuntarily revealed through style. This dissonance between intended character action (within the fiction) and authorial control of the "scene in the mind" – i.e., the author's dramaturgical skill – is a major topic of contemporary literary criticism. Some of the recent sophistication of such criticism could usefully be imported into the theatre, where there is frequent confusion between actions represented *within* the fiction, and actions revealed by the handling of the vision. All "non-realistic" or *presentational* theatre practice is action-based in this way, and in no way "postdramatic" from this perspective.

These are not difficult things to discern or differentiate: one concerns the life of the invented psyches *inside* the story (the characters), the other is our constant confrontation with the dramaturgical skill (and apparent intent) of the author of the play (the playwright) or the "auteur–director" who devises a performance piece. I disagree strongly with those who claim that the author's intent is irrelevant to the realities (and opportunities) inherent in a script. I do agree that a badly written play actually *benefits* from a hostile or critical "reading" of its absurdities and contradictions in performance – one of the vibrant innovations of this age of *re-conceptualization* by gifted "auteur–directors," who take over the aesthetic prerogatives of conventional authors, and re-write each play in production. Those who defend such liberties claim that *all* productions are new interpretations, no matter how faithful they might intend to be. But it is a disingenuous extrapolation to say that because all productions (interpretations) differ from a supposed archetype set down in the script, that therefore all license in "re-writing" *any* script is thereby justified in every production.

In the non-Realist styles in the theatre (i.e., *presentational* styles, sometimes also referred to as "theatricalism") the form is conditioned primarily by the action of the *playwright*, rather than by the supposed fictional action of the *characters* "in" the play. The form still "imitates the action," but the action in question shifts from one lodged *within* the fiction to the action of the *exterior* subject: the playwright composing. Pirandello's *Six Characters in Search of an Author* is the play that made history by making explicit this externalization of the subject action. But the aesthetic shift effectuated in this play had (in 1921) already taken place in painting, as representation shifted with the Impressionists from The Represented to The Representor, to be followed quickly by the decisive break to full abstraction made by Picasso and his contemporaries, as mentioned in the Introduction. Picasso's "imitated action" is his own flamboyant action as a painter. And I have already discussed how the much later coinage "Action Painting" accurately reflects how this aesthetic shift entrenched itself in late twentieth-century abstract art. It is important to note that, in the theatre, an aesthetic shift from Realism to full abstraction leaves intact Aristotle's proposition that the common principle of *all* theatrical styles is the imitation of an *action*. Robert Wilson's action (like Picasso's) is the imitated "subject" of his dramatic forms.

Action; spheres of action; theatres

Action as a term of art is complicated by the difference between "things done" and "things undergone," or roughly speaking, the active and passive forms of action. Stanislavski clearly intended to cover the widest range of experience when he associated *action* with "the life of the human psyche," something Francis Fergusson, in his turn, correlated to Dante's *moto spiritale* or "movement of the spirit," as well as to Aristotle's defining term, *praxis*. All of us experience our own unending action as an essentially *interior* event that, on only *some* occasions, works itself outward to our limbs, which "act" in and on the world. We generally experience The World (which includes other people like ourselves) as exterior, "out there" to be acted on, but also "acting back" on us, jostling us about, impinging either pleasantly or unpleasantly on our experience and on our ongoing interior life. The great practical difficulty of pinning down any particular action (be it a character action in a scene or *the* formal action shaping a play) stems from this fact – experienced by everyone – that *action* has both an internal and an external component.

René Descartes is usually credited with making the duality of Mind/Body distinctions a commonplace of the Modern consciousness, but everyone shares the commonplace experience that *psyche* seems literally to be "inner" (in the head) and that *soma*, our bodies, lie literally "outside," exposed to the world. Both add up – most of the time – to a unitary sense of "One-self." Athletes make the distinction quite concrete by conditioning the body through training and practice, and disciplining the mind to performance pitch via regular disciplines of concentration and stress-management. Actors work analogously on both resources of the Self: inner psychology and "physical culture" – the twin branches of Stanislavski's System of actor training. But the exclusive focus on actors and their needs obscures a greater *theatrical* principle that can be expanded from this metaphorical expression of the Self in spatial forms. The purely *notional* distinction between *psyche*, or "inner" self, and *soma*, or the physical body (subject, incidentally, of renewed interest in recent cultural studies), starts us on a mental road that can fruitfully yield larger and larger spheres of conceptualization: expanding contexts of action. These notional spheres turn out to have very concrete spatial correlatives: they have already been made into cultural "theatres" at each "level" of action. Each *sphere of action* partakes of *idea* and concrete realization in spatial form.

This sort of rumination on *action* leads us to a model of ever-enlarging "spheres of action." Before relating these spheres of action to *theatres* (for this is how *theatres* – "seeing-places" – are in fact defined), I would like to point out that all the existing "fields" (another spatial metaphor) in the Humanities as well as in the Sciences have already been defined for us by reference to "spheres of action," in the very personal-psychological sense discussed above. Figure 2.1 will make these anthropocentric "spheres" (or theatres) clear as I explain.

We start inside the brain-pan of our little figure, where psychology is the specialized study of that "inner realm," the psyche, or the "seat of consciousness." Medicine takes as *its* sphere the immediate next "level": the personal body, and all its organs and biological functions. The body's skin envelope encloses quite literally the "sphere" of medical science and practice. Immediately beyond the Self (that paradoxical unitary–duality of nested *psyche* within its body) comes the sphere of social groupings closest to the self: the immediate biological family, by which we mean wives and husbands, children, brothers, sisters, parents, cousins, in-laws, etc. These kinship groups (and their myriad *domestic* arts) are typically contained within habitations, be they houses, caves, or castles; domestic "hearths" of this sort develop rules of conduct (ethnography, anthropology, mores) which become laws at the next higher level, as families group into tribes, or villages (sociology), and these in turn aggregate into the Polis, or city-state, where the specialized disciplines of law and politics now obtain. Law is unquestionably our most picayune "science" of action: every shade and nuance of *intentionality* is defined and codified within the community,

Anthropomorphic Spheres of Action

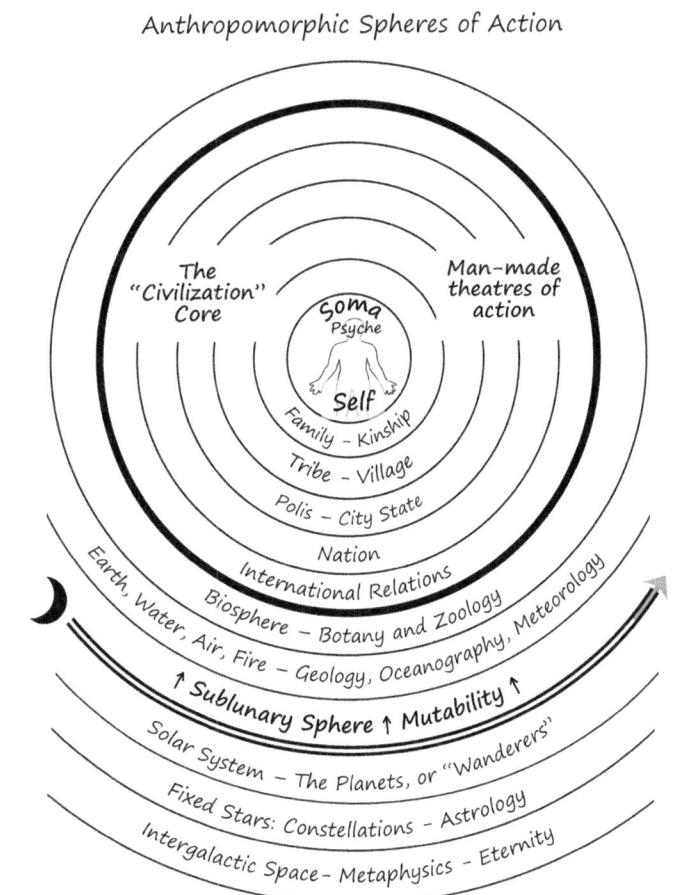

Figure 2.1 Anthropomorphic spheres of action.

with appropriate punishments devised for each degree. This is why "court-room drama" is such an enduring genre, from Aeschylus' *Oresteia* to the latest episode of *Law and Order*. The law is intensely theatrical by nature. Within the smaller "theatre" of the family, the same distinctions are handled intuitively; as the sphere of action *literally* expands, detailed action analysis (and judgment) get more complex.

We have just begun our sketch of concentric "spheres of action," but we have already covered the *ground* or *domain* of 99 percent of the plays ever written and performed in all the known theatres of the world's long history. Think of the *setting* of almost all plays, and you readily see that "rooms" or "buildings" suffice for almost all of them. The Greeks favored an open city space, often before a palace (or seat of government). Yet the concentric "spheres of action" can be continued beyond these conventional settings familiar to us from the plays of our theatre history.

Economics and political science cover the next larger "theatre" of commerce and the interplay between city-states, which grow into our modern geo-political nations and their literal geographical boundaries. International relations (again, a named field) is less amenable to theatrical representation; there are fewer plays portraying this level of geo-politics, but the long history of wars "takes place" at these geographical boundaries and between these nations. The phrase "Theatre of War" is not chosen at random.

Here, in our conceptual diagram (which has literal spatial correlatives) we come to a decisive threshold, one that roughly separates "The Humanities" from the spheres of "The Sciences," but our understanding of drama (things done and things undergone) continues to operate into these outer spheres. Beyond the "Humanities," or human-manipulated structures of civilized life (preoccupation *par excellence* of our theatre as a cultural instrument) our spheres of action continue to grow spatially in scale and extent – and they continue to be both conceptual *and* literal locations of action – spatially larger and larger named entities.

The world of nature encircles all our personal and political circles, and we call the enveloping realm of all living plants and animals, our "biosphere." Botany and Zoology are nature's named sciences, and this biosphere is, in its turn, inscribed inside (and supported by) the physical habitat of the earth, its seas and land and atmosphere. Geology and other "Earth Sciences" operate in and enclose this space, and we are increasingly conscious of the drama unfolding in that "theatre." Beyond earth, the orbit of the moon has formed an important real and also psychological divide throughout mankind's long history. The moon is ever-changing to the eye, and it is the most mobile and various object in the sky. The sun, by contrast, is steady and reliable. The moon's orbit defines the Sublunary World we live in, where our destinies and dramas unfold relentlessly in time. It encloses the ancient elements of earth, water, air, and fire and here everything is doomed (like the moon) to everlasting mutability and change, endless cycles of birth, growth to maturity, decay, and death. The sun measures days, the moon months; both together regulate the year cycle that is the basis of all organic life.

But we are not done with our anthropocentric spheres of action. The planets of our solar system have always been studied as unique in the night sky because, unlike the fixed stars, the planets are "wanderers" who exhibit baffling periodic recursions and reversals into retrograde motions that have made people think they have minds of their own. They are named after gods as a result. And a study called astrology is an ancient effort to extrapolate *action* and agency even "out there," well beyond human reach in the supralunar spheres. Beyond the solar system, and still included in astronomy, lie the fixed stars and their configurations into constellations, which migrate majestically through the year cycle, but apparently never change. Beyond the night sky stars and their mapped shapes lies "deep" space. Note that at this level, the imagined entity is actually named – tellingly – "space" – the naked and unadorned word of our expanding metaphor itself. Intergalactic space, even today, conjures ideas of divinity, infinity, and ultimate ends: theology and metaphysics. Our entire exercise here is meant to demonstrate how deeply rooted our instinct for naming our perceptual theatres is. These spheres are rigorously anthropocentric. They all function, in the human experience and imagination, as theatres of action.

When working in the theatre it is always useful to re-examine our conventions. Craft-consciousness demands a sophisticated awareness of the formal mapping we are engaged in when we freight our playing area with meaning (a conscious process). All real theatres are arenas for representing *assigned* spheres of action. It never hurts to be highly conscious, as artists, of our range of assignable values, and it is endlessly valuable to see that *action* is the term governing all our choices.

Language as symbolic action: Kenneth Burke's enduring legacy

The insurgent performance elements are generally lost or unrecorded in the book form of a play. For those who are in everyday contact with the theatre and not just books, there is a huge and self-evident shift in consciousness between mere language (words, words, words) and the far more vivid and dynamic physical "stuff" that constitutes the experience of performance. The physical body in space, its appearance, the play of light on it and on its vestments, the cut and trim of costumes, all these are unmistakably foregrounded at the expense of the distant "subject matters" that lurk like stowaways inside the "textuality" that has such disproportionate prominence in the script. Those words (that "literature") will eventually come into play, but only when an overwhelmingly larger event is set in motion. The words will be but a part of a much larger whole. The apparent balance between words and *other things* is reversed in practice from what it appears in the script.

In literary terms, this shift from *action* to what literary culture calls the *logos* is a shift in existential register. Kenneth Burke has called our attention usefully to the *symbology* inherent in literary experience (Burke, 1969). Language, he points out, is *symbolic action*. As such, it differs ontologically from "live action" as performed by actors. Every actor demonstrates his or her degree of talent precisely along and across this line of demarcation. But the *literary fallacy*, as it might be called in the theatre, is provoked and perpetuated by the way books are printed, bound, and used. There is a notoriously wide disparity between the "book experience" of plays and the sensuous experiential complex of live performance. Properly discerning the relevant *action* behind any passage of words is the fastest way to become fully competent in the theatre.

The dramaturgy advocated here depends on re-focusing the professional's mind until what is most apparent to the attentive artist is the play's phenomenological presence as a rhythmic time-sculpture, something crafted as a careful succession of planned durations. That these time-beads are filled with words is a partial truth about most plays. The rest of the truth is that the time-beads are also filled with spectacle, sound, silences, movement, stillnesses, and the powerful animal presence of the performers – including any and all legible actions the actors embody and convey. But in our day, the words have a disproportionate advantage when it comes to captivating the audience's attention. On the printed page, the words seem in fact to be the whole play. It is a common misperception about playscripts. Spoken aloud, the words fall into better proportion to the other elements, but even fully sounded, the articulated logos retains a great part of the habitual advantage it enjoys on the page. But if words (and literature) consistently distort our full perception of dramatic form, Kenneth Burke's elaborate "symbology" can help re-focus the professional artist's proper emphasis in the theatre, by teaching theatre artists to heed the enormous difference between the deep tectonic actions (praxis) embodied in the live actors set aprowl on the stage, and the fog of symbolic action and apparent "meaning" sprayed into the consciousness of the audience by the inevitable and incessant chatter that parallels action. In the end, the action is the thing – not the words.

References

Burke, K. (1969) *A Grammar of Motives*. Berkeley: University of California Press. (Originally published 1945.)

Butcher, S.H. and Aristotle (1961) *Aristotle's Poetics*. (Translated 1895, Introduction by F. Fergusson, 1961). New York: Hill and Wang.

Cole, T. and Rapoport, I.M. (1995) "The Work of the Actor" by I.M. Rapoport, in *Acting: A Handbook of the Stanislavski Method*, collected by T. Cole. New York: Three Rivers Press. (Reprint of 1947 edition. "The Work of the Actor" was originally published in Theatre Workshop, 1936.)

Dewey, J. (1934) *Art as Experience.* New York: Capricorn Books.

Fergusson, F. (1957) *The Human Image in Dramatic Literature.* New York: Doubleday.

Fyfe, W.H. and Aristotle (1932) *The Poetics,* in vol. XXIII of the Loeb Classical Library *Aristotle.* London: William Heinemann Ltd.

Hammond, W.A. and Aristotle (1902) *Aristotle's Psychology (De Amina and Parva Naturalia).* London: Swan Sonnenschein & Co.

Hett, W.S. and Aristotle (1957) *On the Soul,* in vol. VIII of the Loeb Classical Library *Aristotle.* London: William Heinemann Ltd.

Hornby, R. (2000) *The End of Acting.* New York: Applause.

Stanislavski, K. (1980) *An Actor Prepares.* Translated by E.R. Hapgood, 1937. London: Methuen. (Originally published 1936.)

3   Production Dramaturgy

"A place at the table": blueprint for Production Dramaturgy

What is known as "Production Dramaturgy" is the art of being useful and effectively influential during the actual staging of a particular play. A practical dramaturg has many roles to play during a production, all of them clear and orderly if the principles of dramaturgy are firmly kept in mind. Once it is well understood, for instance, that "dramaturgy" is the art of "arranging the incidents" – whether the event so arranged be *King Lear* or a dog-and-pony act – we can talk of the "dramaturgy" of a poem, of a good joke, of a street busker's ten-minute sidewalk show – even the dramaturgy of a good meal, or of a hot date. But if we are talking of the dramaturgy of a play that is about to be put into production, we are talking about the essential core of an artistic entity that exists only via a complex process. A play put into production is about to absorb vast resources: a lot of money, to start with, but also large amounts of time and imaginative energy. For such expenditure of resources to be worthwhile, it is imperative that the dramaturgy (the arrangements of the incidents) be gotten right, just as it is imperative in the case of music-making that the *music* be gotten right. The purpose of the special discipline known as "Production Dramaturgy" is thus to ensure the integrity of the production – something that goes beyond just enriching and enhancing the play by enlarging and illuminating the creative context within which it is staged.

Production Dramaturgy is performed first by grasping the *core* of the artifact, and secondarily by bringing a digestible amount of relevant, stimulating, and accurate information and insight into play at every stage of production. Obviously, there will be varying degrees of appropriate "enrichment," depending on the particular project.

Given that the person designated as the production dramaturg is a collaborator in a creative process, her or his role has to enjoy the respect and freedom accorded any artist. In plain practical terms, the production dramaturg needs to be given a place at the table – a literal figure when it comes to sitting at a director's side at planning sessions and in the rehearsal hall, but also a metaphorical figure for being allowed full access to and full participation in the creative process. The director must of course remain the final arbiter and decision maker, and that necessarily entails remaining the principal communicator with the actors and the designers – that is the director's job – but beyond the obvious responsibilities of providing clear artistic leadership, there is little point in excessive subordination of the production dramaturg. There is a distinct need to establish careful procedural protocols (who speaks to whom when, and of what) but these protocols should not be so conceived and enforced as to suppress the production dramaturg's freedom or desire to contribute ideas to a production. Production dramaturgs have sometimes been described as "best friends" to a production, and though the label is not rigorous enough for the full range of professional disciplines that a trained dramaturg must bring into play, it does accurately suggest the deep bond of trust and respect (free of rivalry) that is an ideal of Production Dramaturgy.

The skills needed for Production Dramaturgy

There are three types of skills involved in Production Dramaturgy:

1 Analytical acumen, which entails close study, thinking, and deep reflection. A distinctive kind of *insight* is the hallmark of analytical dramaturgical work, and it is generated (in contrast to other dramaturgical information) by the individual dramaturg in communion with the playscript.
2 Knowledge, supported by education and research skills. Research requires scholarly discipline, clarity of mind, orderliness, and perseverance. It also implies wide collateral reading and a knowledge of where to look for sources. These skills and disciplines (often disparaged in theatre circles as academic) generate *information* from outside sources such as socio-political history, literary history, biography, production history, scholarly studies, etc.
3 Communication skills, which means writing and speaking ability. These rhetorical skills are required to collate, condense, and dispense information and insight.

Tact and common sense, and a certain knack for making oneself persuasive, are as important to the production dramaturg as are the research skills usually associated with literary and academic expertise. A good dramaturg needs to be a good writer, but it doesn't hurt to cultivate a quick rhetorical flair as well, and to retain a conscious place for an easy sense of humor. Dramaturgs have to train for what I call "the Dramaturgical Moment": a sudden opening in an ongoing rehearsal or during a planning meeting when the natural flow of multi-layered conversation suddenly gives the floor to the production dramaturg – a fact is needed, a "reading" of the play or of a scene is called for, historical context is suddenly sought – it can be any pretext, and it usually comes without warning; the dramaturg must be ready, or the "moment" goes by unused, and is therefore lost. When a dramaturg responds fully and with full participation in the flow of production ideas, then a confidence builds up in that team member's utility and reliability in the creative process. A dramaturg who fluffs his or her "moments" will not be given many more in the future development of the production – and remember that most productions move swiftly day by day and hour by hour. Time is short (and expensive) in theatre production, and planning meetings and rehearsals must yield significant and visible progress all the time. A production dramaturg, to be effective, has to enter into the real-time traffic in ideas and bold gambits that is the actor's and the director's stock-in-trade. No one wants to be slowed down in his or her work by a ponderous "literary type" who is used to the deliberative rhythms of the study or the library – or worse yet, the lecture hall. You don't want to hear "I'll look that up and get back to you," you want to hear an accurate and deft response from someone who has already done her homework, and is fully informed *now*, because she has anticipated that the needed information *would* be needed.

Finally, a fully trained dramaturg should be a good essay writer. This essential skill lies at the other end of a spectrum of communication skills from the rhetorical Dramaturgical Moment described above. The one requires a quick and deft verbal response, the other should be comprehensive, elegant, and formal. Effective dramaturgs need to respond in planning meetings and in rehearsals, but it is also the production dramaturg's job to supply informative, accurate, and lively essays for newsletters, programs, and archival records. These natural extensions of completed Production Dramaturgy should be married to the quick repartee of real-time response in the rehearsal hall. The best way to get good at it is to be thoroughly prepared (the same requirement behind good directing work). The professional dramaturg should be quick, useful, fun to be around (a conscious responsibility), and he or she should also be planning at every moment how to leave a distinguished written record of all that has passed and is passing on his or her watch.

The core: the full dramaturgical workup

Once the role of the production dramaturg is understood, the following outline can usefully guide the dramaturg through the preparatory phase of his/ her work. A full dramaturgical workup is a thorough cycle of analysis and research, and it accompanies and guides a basic production sequence that I will discuss below, with examples, in the Process section of this chapter.

There are two main categories in the full dramaturgical workup:

1 those things for which the source is **the play script itself**, and ...
2 those areas where sources of information lie **outside the play**.

Of these, the play script itself is by far the most important, but a dramaturg must recognize that the script is also the specific area of expertise of the director and the actors: *their* dramaturgical skills and talent are focused primarily there. If a dramaturg is usefully to *supplement* the skills and expertise of actors and directors, he or she must seek and work territory just outside the habitual focus of fellow artists. In practice this means concentrating on the large underlying structures of the script (i.e., the *plot*) and on areas of extensive research outside the script. A basic rule distinguishes dramaturgy from academic literary studies, and that rule dictates that any *textual* scrutiny must be guided by an understanding that what is printed as "text" is not the artifact we are studying; our play-text is a score for a *performance* which all our skills of analysis will try to envision (and understand) and all our techniques of research will try to enrich, supplement, and illuminate. As a consequence, there are different rules of engagement for literary critics and production dramaturgs. The four types of research sources *outside* the play (ranked in what follows in a suggested order of their importance) are the special domain of the production dramaturg, and this specialization should serve the production: active directors and actors just don't have enough time (given their many other duties with respect to each production) to carry out the kind of thorough collateral research that a good dramaturg should provide.

The full dramaturgical workup

I **The play itself (analysis)**

1 **Summarizing the gist, or "backstory" of the play**
This includes specification of the setting, period, and milieu of the play; the principal characters, their relationships and the governing idea of the "backstory" – assuming there is one. This first-cut overview provides a synoptic "handle" on the play.

2   Plot analysis
This formal analysis is centered on the preparation of a plot-bead diagram of the play; it requires careful differentiation of the plot/ artifact from the distraction of the "story." Beads and Hinges are identified throughout the performance event. The architecture of the artifact is structured into the plot.

3   The action of the play
This involves a beat-by-beat, scene-by-scene, act-by-act discernment of the *motivational* structure of all plot elements. Discovering *the action* of all the "parts" of a play (including "The Action" governing the whole) is the principal work of the actors and their director. It is possible to discern "The Action" of non-representational (non-realistic) plays; the "histrionic sensibility" (akin to an "ear for music") is the key to action analysis. Dramaturgs typically refocus *action* work on the shape of the *plot*.

4   Text issues: translation, cuts, and text editing
Dramaturgs assist in the selection and preparation of acting editions; selection and/or preparation of translations when needed; judicious editing of the performance text, including cutting, transpositions, details of diction, word meaning, style. This is all close, detailed work, requiring precision, knowledge of the plot, and patience.

II   Sources outside the play (research)

1   Sources of the play
Research into the literary and/or historical source and setting of the story–subject. This will usually include detailed historical research beyond what the author knew and researched, but it should at the very least include the primary sources used by the dramatic author. What was once "contemporary" source material becomes an occasion for historical research within a few years.

2   The author of the play
Research into the socio-historical occasion of the *writing* of the play (to be compared and contrasted to the socio-historical occasion of the present production). This includes the personal biographical circumstances of the writing of the play, including shaping biographical influences, an overview of the playwright's *œuvre* (patterns of style and key signature of the author), assessment and appreciation of the playwright's relevance and success, which amounts to an assessment of the artist's connection to his or her historical moment.

3   Production history
Research into previous stage versions and treatments of the play, both recently and in the more distant past, both locally and in other parts of the world.

4   Survey of the critical and scholarly literature
These materials are much like the dramaturg's own analyses of the play script, only they are based on the literary and speculative criticism of other people, usually literary scholars (since they routinely publish their studies of plays). The "indispensable" critics must be winnowed from the rest, and their opinions and findings brought to the attention of the artistic team. Frequently, a director will want to adopt a critical *bias* for the production, in which case supporting documents are needed to convey a chosen paradigm of interpretation.

A working dramaturg can construct his or her assignments from this outline alone, for once given a clear orientation to what is needed, the work is largely self-guided, with each discovery and insight leading to the next – as is typical in all research activity. With the development of a national dramaturg's archive online – an idea frequently discussed at Literary Managers and Dramaturgs of the Americas (L.M.D.A.) meetings – "full workups" by other dramaturgs in other theatres would increasingly supplement the available library materials, which are mainly the work of academic literary critics and historians, and frequently lack a specifically theatrical orientation. Inevitably, the work of critics and production dramaturgs will vary in methodology and in quality, so dramaturgical research (like all library work) depends on an acquired ability to discern and select quality work. All thoughtful critical writing, however, will help focus the mind and serve as an aid to reflection. For many practical dramaturgs, the sheer volume of accumulated materials can be daunting and off-putting. But it is worth learning how to review and evaluate the literature, for that small percentage of criticism that is brilliant needs to be found and made available to directors, designers, and actors.

   In practice, theatre artists tend to be hungry for enrichment material (like historical detail) but wary of extraneous interpretations by academics. They are generally right on this score. A good dramaturg will be very careful about interpreting a play: it is not the dramaturg's principal work to do so. Conversely, it will be very hard, once a dramaturg's proper work has been thoroughly done, not to have incidentally generated a persuasive and authoritative reading of a play. This reading should emerge as early in the production as possible, and it should play itself out in the minds and imaginations of fellow artists naturally, influencing where it may, and blending seamlessly into the rhythm of the work. Correspondingly, it is frequently important for a dramaturg to leave behind a favorite "reading" or interpretation of a play once a decision *not to use it* has been made by the director. But that gets us into process, and the ways in which a full dramaturgical workup blends into and supports a full production will next be examined in detail, with supporting examples at each stage.

The process

Prologue/overview

The production of existing finished plays invariably begins with reading and understanding the script. This leads in turn to preliminary breakdowns and analyses that will inform all treatment decisions, including design meetings where specifications and requirements of the play must be accurately outlined, and all options and decisions vetted, revised (with budget considerations governing all possibilities), and finally settled. All well-trained designers do their own research in these dramaturgical areas, but it is a good idea for the production dramaturg to monitor the process closely, and to compare his findings to those of the designers. The *core* of a play has to be firmly apprehended at this earliest of production stages, and it is good practice to ask the production dramaturg for a "reading" of the play at these preliminary design meetings. We are talking here not just of a "first impression," but of an understanding of the script that is informed by close structural and thematic analysis. What is this play *really* about, and what are the possible avenues of stress and focus available to the production? How has this play been understood and interpreted in the past, and how does it strike us now? Good directors who know how to take full advantage of their assembled collaborators will cast the net wide at this stage in the process, and – if time permits – they will indulge in a period of reflection and debate, scheduling deliberate and well-managed sessions for discussion and creative brainstorming. After a time of thorough exploration of possibilities, the director and his/her team will then determine the "take this time," meaning the way the play will be handled and interpreted in this particular production. After that is determined, all subsequent preparation for rehearsals has a central focus, and the relevance of dramaturgical *enrichment* can be swiftly established.

Dramaturgical input normally continues in the rehearsal hall throughout rehearsals, but it also is useful in the preparation of publicity, marketing strategies, audience development, and associated educational programs. Just before opening, the production dramaturg has pretty much done his or her work, but during final technical rehearsals and preview performances, the dramaturg is a good candidate for serving as an "in-house critic," or a friend of the production who anticipates audience (and critic) response while something can still be done about performance detail. Such work is typically done during a "preview" week, while the play is performed before an audience in alternation with continuing daily rehearsals. In what follows, we will review all the stages of the production process, to review at each stage the full range of support Production Dramaturgy is capable of providing to a well-managed production.

Process (1): reading the play

The first thing to do, of course, is to read the play. The play (its script) in most situations governs all the production work that follows. There are legal obligations involved in following the traditional practice of being governed by the script. In the case of a living playwright, or of one whose estate still holds copyright over the author's play, these legal obligations are very real, and they will be enforced if they are not respected. But even without the imperatives dictated by law, there are powerful ethical and aesthetic reasons to heed the requirements of the script. The script holds the *form* of the play, and distorting or otherwise mishandling this form *adulterates* the original artifact. Whether or not one should *respect* that form is a debate that can be relegated to matters of *style*, but for the purposes of this chapter, suffice it to state that departures from the scripted form should be *choices* deliberately made, not clumsy errors made inadvertently.

At the American Repertory Theatre, I made a routine practice of asking my dramaturgy and directing students to read a playscript seven times – a practice that if done conscientiously, can be starkly illuminating. The pensum of reading a script seven times functions didactically as a sort of spiritual exercise akin to certain disciplines of meditation. It is a very difficult thing to make oneself do. But confronting this odd fact (why *should* it be difficult?) is not a bad starting point for developing a professional attitude toward a playscript. Our everyday criterion for familiarity – "I've read that" – is inadequate for the kind of information that is contained (or implied) in a script.

The plain fact of the matter is that it is the imagination that determines whether or not one can manage seven re-readings of a playscript. Until the dramatic imagination (what Francis Fergusson called *the histrionic sensibility*) has been activated and engaged, the repetition of readings will be a sterile pensum, a process excruciatingly boring because the mind has shut itself off from anything it doesn't already know. If one assumes that the stuff on the surface (the words) are the "thing" we have been asked to read (the play), then of course re-reading is mind-numbingly redundant. One has to learn to read for something well beyond the words, and the dutiful performance of the required seven readings (try it, dear reader) will usually trigger the discovery of the large imaginative realm behind any good playscript.

Process (2): summarizing the gist of the play, backstory, and return to the plot

It is a good idea to get a story summary out in the open swiftly, if for no other reason than to clear the decks for an unclouded distinction between story and plot. It is also a good idea to get story elements in hand at the outset because story is the red herring that most frequently obscures a craftsman's view of the artifact we call a play. Yet on first or second reading, a story summary is the easiest "handle" one can get on a play. Let's take a specific example, say Gotthold Lessing's *Minna von Barnhelm* (1767), a play that theatre historians constantly tell us is important, but one which has never managed to sustain much attention in the English-speaking world. The play (Lessing, 1972) provides a useful example for several reasons that go to the heart of Production Dramaturgy. *Minna von Barnhelm*, for all its reputed importance, has never spontaneously fired the imagination of English-speaking theatre people. No one in America is likely to have seen a production of it. Yet the play remains, for some reason, an established classic of the German stage – one that is frequently revisited in German theatres. Why this disparity? What are we missing about this play?

Because it is so unfamiliar here, it will be clear how even the most basic questions need to be asked and answered before we tackle more deeply cultural ones. Once we have conducted a full dramaturgical workup on the play, we will see how added lateral context might re-awaken contemporary interest in it – in fact, the deeper layers of Lessing's old comedy lead directly back to a contemporary and still widely misunderstood American work: Robert Wilson's and Heiner Müller's so-called "Cologne Section" of *the CIVIL warS*. This postmodern masterpiece, first produced in Germany (the city of Köln, which is known as Cologne in English) and re-staged at the American Repertory Theatre in 1985, was the unanimous first choice of the Pulitzer drama committee for that year's prize. But because of its unconventional dramaturgy (chiefly the absence of a conventional script) *the CIVIL warS* was denied the prize. What might *Minna von Barnhelm* have to do with the postmodern controversy over *the CIVIL warS*? The connection is certainly not obvious at the surface level, but once unearthed by dramaturgical analysis and research, it runs deep, and is a good example of the type of untapped contemporary energies that remain inaccessible and unappreciated without conscientious dramaturgy.

A first order of questions takes the following common-sense form: what is *Minna von Barnhelm* about? Who is in it? Where does it take place? When? What's the principal action? What *experience* frames the play – i.e., what determines its beginning and end? Here are some down-and-dirty dramaturgical answers: "It's about a discharged army officer who is scrambling to make ends meet while he awaits a judgment on accusations of fiscal malfeasance lodged against him at the War Ministry." "It's about a rich young noblewoman who is searching for a reluctant lover who has inexplicably flown the coop." "It's about an innkeeper who has evicted a non-paying guest in order to accommodate a better prospective client." It is, of course, about all three of the above narrative strands interlaced into a lively comedy. For someone who knows nothing about *Minna von Barnhelm*, such answers provide a useful first-cut orientation. But the gist of any play (its *story*) usually misleads natural human interest into a non-artisanal attitude toward a script. This is where the discipline of *principles* of dramaturgy needs to guide the dramaturg, and shifting from story concerns (and interests) to plot analysis is the swiftest way to keep on track if what one is heading toward is a theatre production.

The distinction between plot and story is worth elaborating. Plot analysis is an immediate assessment of the *form* of the actual play: what happens first, what happens after that, etc. The plot-bead diagram introduced in Chapter 1 is a proven technique for concentrating the mind on this formal object, which is of immediate practical utility. But the natural "unprofessional" or amateur tendency of most readers of plays is to follow the gist of the play, and its story content, into elaborations of *narrative* detail. By far the most compelling red herring of any narrative is what, in the film industry, is usefully termed its "backstory." Backstory is essentially the detailed antecedents for the action of the play – all the imaginary stuff that *precedes*, in "narrative time," the events that actually constitute a play or a movie. These imaginary events are seldom part of the play (and that is the most obvious reason not to get sidetracked into them). Yet human interest in stories leads to an irrepressible natural curiosity into backstory, whether we like it or not. This is what gives rise to the notorious problem of *exposition* in play scripts. The fact that exposition is always a problem (with varyingly satisfying solutions) should help illuminate the distinction between story and plot.

The *plot*, in practical terms, needs to get on with itself, but the snag of *story* retards that action, and forces most playwrights to satisfy essentially extraneous demands before recovering the freedom to proceed with their play. Ibsen, for one, followed Sophocles' paramount example (*Oedipus*

Tyrannos) in constructing several plays (*Ghosts* is his best example of this) on a plot structure that systematically unearths backstory. The principal action of *Ghosts* is reflected directly in the sequence of its plot: the *ostensible* action of the play (the dedication of the new orphan's home) is constantly retarded and finally scuttled by the relentless, almost nightmarish encroachment of re-emerging backstory (the past) on the plot (the present). This allies the play (and all plays like it) with the fundamental procedure of Freudian psychoanalysis, the action of which is to root back in the past, reconstructing a narrative understanding of "what happened," in order to achieve some current objective in the present. In Sophocles' *Oedipus Tyrannos*, the seeking action is deliberate, and it is meant to "cure the plague in Thebes." In Ibsen's *Ghosts*, the resurgence of the past is inadvertent. In Ibsen's related play, *The Wild Duck*, the buried past is brought up deliberately by a troublemaker (Gregers Werle) who precipitates the death of a child by his reckless meddling in other people's lives. Gregers destabilizes the present by injecting the past into it – a striking demonstration of the power of backstory over plot, but also a good reminder that almost *all* plays begin by destabilizing a situation which must then regain a certain equilibrium before the play is complete.

If we return to the example of *Minna von Barnhelm*, filling in the backstory requires some careful re-reading of the script and patient attention (and note-taking). The dramaturg should, indeed, be among the first to assemble such pertinent facts from the script, but the dramaturg *especially* should avoid being distracted from the play itself by such ferreting about for an essentially *literary* idea. That is why I advocate shifting attention early on to the preparation of a plot-bead diagram, rather than to the elaboration of backstory. This point should be driven home by the fact that the details of the backstory are frequently scattered almost randomly throughout a script, and the *form* of the play (its most important artistic feature) has almost to be ignored to re-construct backstory. There is no way to determine *a priori* where in the script the key story-facts will have been tucked away. The backstory of *Minna von Barnhelm*, for example, is doled out only fitfully throughout the five acts of the play, and it takes two or three attentive readings of the play to assemble the following elaboration of its backstory:

> The main character is not the title character, Minna von Barnhelm (who makes her first appearance at the top of the second act), but the de-commissioned army officer, Major von Tellheim. After serving with distinction in an unnamed war (fighting what enemy for what state?), the Major has fallen foul of some damaging (but as it turns out false) accusations that have discredited him. He is owed a great deal

of money by the War Ministry, but he is accused instead of embezzlement or misappropriation of funds, and he has been forced to pledge that he will not leave the jurisdiction of the royal court until the disposition of his case. As he waits under a cloud of imputed disgrace, he grows increasingly destitute. He has taken up residency in a modest inn in the capital, but after many months, he is falling behind in the payment of his bill. A devoted army buddy has tracked the Major down and induced him to accept a stash of money, but Major von Tellheim is so punctilious on the subject of money that he never resorts to this ready cash for his own growing needs. The plot begins when Minna von Barnhelm arrives in town, looking for her fiancé – the same Major Tellheim – who has inexplicably disappeared from her life. The comedy begins with the absurd coincidence that Minna's first stop in town is the very inn where Tellheim has been lodging, and the compounded coincidence that the landlord chooses to evict his non-paying guest (Tellheim, of course) from his room in order to accommodate the newly arrived Minna, a young lady of obvious wealth and station (who is likely to prove a better paying customer).

This is a complicated story, and most people would confusingly mischaracterize it as the "plot" of the play. But the plot is something else entirely. The backstory sketched out above would be extremely useful printed in the theatre's program, because it would, in this case, greatly enhance everyone's enjoyment of the *plot* by relieving a certain amount of confusion and stress over following exposition on the fly. Many established classics are more enjoyable precisely because their basic "story" content is well known. Many seasoned theatregoers will take pains, for instance, to review the basic *story* before attending a Shakespeare production. It is revealing how hard it can be, when dealing with an unfamiliar play, to be absolutely accurate in reconstructing backstory, in getting it right. But the plot, by contrast, is right there in front of us: what happens first, what happens after that, and after that, what next? In our dramaturgy seminars at Harvard, we repeatedly sat down – eight or ten of us, who had all read the play several times – to get the backstory sorted from the plot. Invariably, as we worked, we would hit some snag in getting the story down: some detail could not be remembered, some twist in the story was not clear. After diligent search, sure enough, we could usually find the stray narrative pieces – but often, too (especially in minor plays), we would find unfilled gaps, imaginative blunders, and even irreconcilable contradictions.

The plot, by contrast, is always directly accessible: the play begins with *something*: in this case an early morning scene in the parlor of the inn.

First, we see a fitfully sleeping servant waking up from a dream; in the dream, the servant imagines he is beating up the innkeeper. Next, the innkeeper arrives in person, and tries to mollify the servant by offering him free *schnapps* as they review their quarrel of the night before. The play is launched... what happens after that? Major von Tellheim appears and instructs his servant to pay their outstanding bill and find lodgings elsewhere. The innkeeper remonstrates that, although he *has* reassigned the Major's room to a new guest, he has made another room available to his longstanding military lodger. But the alternate room is not good enough, and the offended Major has decided to lodge elsewhere in future. These "events" in the order in which they occur, add up (as the plot-bead diagram will make clear) to the *form* of the play – i.e., its identity as a work of art in time. It is, in this conventional play, *incidentally* based on a story.

Further differentiation of backstory from plot: Ionesco's The Bald Soprano

Backstory, once elaborated, typically takes us narratively to the point where the play begins – another proof that it is never really a part of the plot of a play. Eugène Ionesco's *The Bald Soprano* caused a sensation in its time (1950) in large part *because* the play has no decipherable backstory, in the conventional sense; yet the plot of *The Bald Soprano* can be easily sketched in a plot-bead diagram (see Figure 3.1). This absurdist play's exact form in time is just as accessible to the dramaturg as is the form of a conventional play. And just as in any conventional play, the plot provides the guiding principle for *producing* the play; furthermore, all the play's meanings emerge from the *plot*, while "meaning" has been skillfully and deliberately stripped from the *story*. Ionesco made his mark as a playwright by audaciously inventing a *style* of drama that wittily exploits the interplay between plot and the conventional *expectation* of a related backstory. This innovative style was dubbed (by the critic Martin Esslin) "Theatre of the absurd" (Esslin, 1961) and this catchphrase accurately epitomized the style's complete *in*dependence from the traditional, logical connection usually woven between backstory and plot. In order to work as a style, the audience must "catch on" to what is missing, and they can only catch on if they are *expecting* the plot to continue a backstory. If an audience fails to appreciate the way in which plot and backstory *cannot* be made to match, they miss the humor that drives the play.

Ionesco was completely aware of the way backstory traditionally infiltrates plot – i.e., quite unnaturally – and he consistently mocked the way explanatory narrative matter is larded into the plot sequence in the guise of "exposition." It is this unchallenged *dependency* on coherent backstory

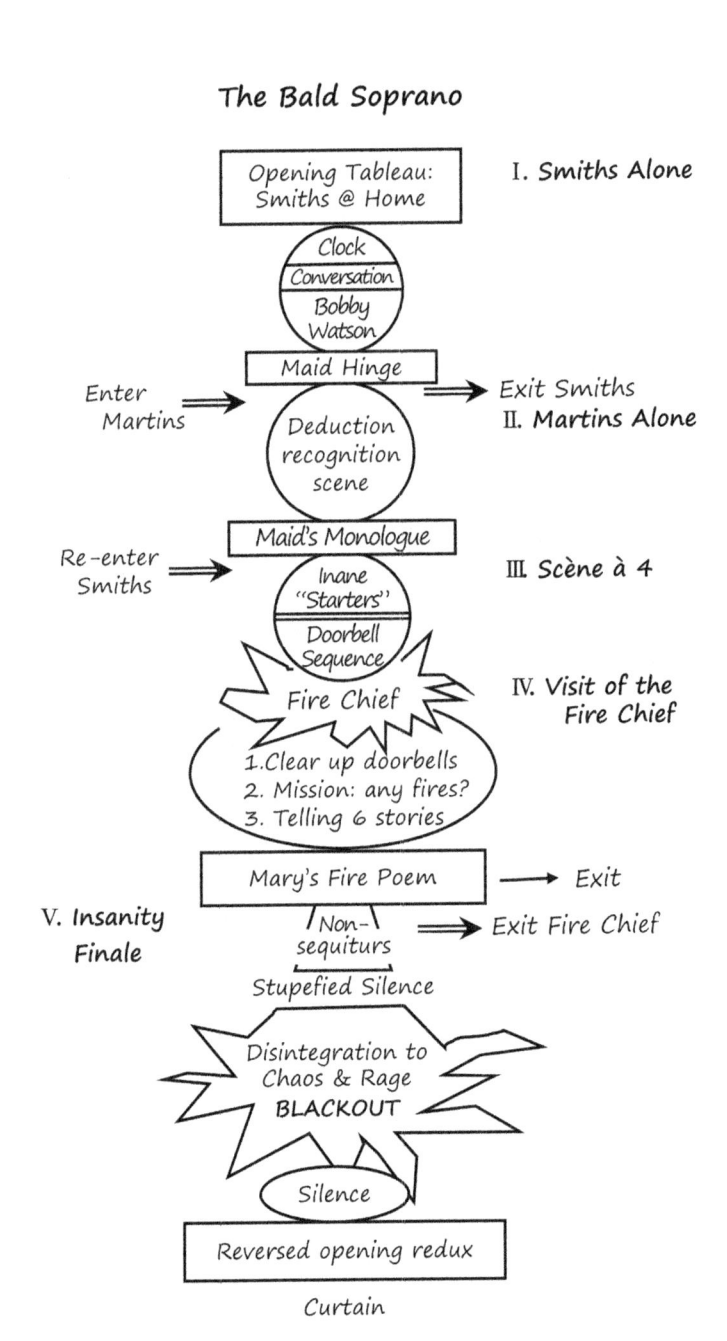

Figure 3.1 Plot-bead diagram of Eugène Ionesco's *The Bald Soprano.*

that has enervated *avant-garde* artists since the end of the nineteenth century, when they did their best to make the convention collapse. Manifesto after manifesto announced the collapse of logical concatenation as a principle of dramaturgy (especially after the social disruption of the first world war) but plays continued to defy the manifestos. Most plays continued – and continue to this day – to be wedded to a narrative frame, however carefully hidden it might be. Actors and designers and their director "dress" their imaginative workspace (the way a painter "dresses" a canvas with a foundation on which to paint – or the way a sculptor "dresses" a rock preliminary to sculpting work). This dressing is backstory – even in the case of *The Bald Soprano*. Ionesco's play is famous because it set out to eviscerate the basic conventions (and relevance) of all prior "parlor plays," and it succeeded. It also perfectly captured the "stupified silence" of postwar Europe emerging from the nightmare of mass slaughter in World War II. Conventions of everyday life no longer made any sense, and a nameless fury lay beneath all conventional forms.

This backdrop for action is the "context" the dramaturg should help unearth and make explicit as soon as possible in a production. Once this work is done, the dramaturg should carefully trace the *plot* that weaves itself across this background. Every play Samuel Beckett ever wrote is constructed on this model: a plot traces across a coherent (but often hidden) backstory. Bertolt Brecht never wrote a scene without a backstory. And every theatre-composition of Robert Wilson's of which I am aware can be made tractable by the same formal analysis: an unfolding sequence in "real-time" (by which I mean theatre-time) plays over an allusive field of backstory – and Wilson's "fields" are always thematically deeply coherent. In Wilson's work, the plot is generally *not* devised in order to help the spectator piece together backstory, and this has frustrated conventional theatregoers. But plot analysis is still the fastest route to discerning the idea behind each Wilson work.

If we return to the first act of *Minna von Barnhelm* we can readily recognize that the opening scenes are devised in order to facilitate exposition; but they also launch the action of the play, and that launched action (the Major is moving out of the inn) is far more important than the elements of revealed backstory, which are in fact few in the first act. The awkward *necessity* of exposition is a major issue in playwriting. There was a day and age when flaws in story logic were considered serious demerits that diminished one's respect for the playwright who had committed them. Modernism broke with the tradition of demanding logical story continuity from play crafters, and postmodernism has made a fetish of discontinuity and narrative incoherence. Now *postdramatic* is supposed to have liberated theatre composers completely from all concatenations. Ironically, the best defense of such strategies in the arts is that such narrative incoherence better reflects modern reality: that it is contemporary experience itself that *justifies* incoherence and absurdist *non-sequitur*. That critical debate has yet to play itself out.

Process (3): plot-bead diagrams (script breakdown and analysis)

With story-summaries out of the way, the production dramaturg should prepare a succinct plot-bead diagram as a permanent contribution to everyone concerned with the production. This is time-consuming and thus must be done early. The actors in the play and their director may seem like the most obviously concerned, but the production's designers and stage managers also govern their every move by the specifics of the plot. These technical theatre departments already use the word "plot" in exactly its technical sense: they talk of lighting plots, which are exact sequences of cues, of sound plots, which are sequential lists of occasions for sound effects, music, and special acoustic manipulations – and we have corresponding costume plots (which costumes are needed in which scenes, in what sequence), properties plots, set-change plots etc. Everywhere, specific work assignments are governed by the plot: the lists and duties of prop crews and stagehands; costume plots and change schedules; the sequencing of sound cues on data discs and the complex elaborations of light cue programs; house management procedures and the staffing needs of concession stands are all governed by the rigors of the plot. Everyone in the theatre has to coordinate around the specifics of what will actually be *taking place* – an exact sequence in time – in the theatre on the occasion of each performance. The *subject matter* of the play, or the *story* it may tell are, by contrast, relatively incidental.

Let's look in detail at a plot-bead diagram of the first act of *Minna von Barnhelm* (Figures 3.2a and 3.2b). A cursory structural analysis of the act reveals nine "scenes" in a row as the basic string-in-time that makes up the act, and a first cut at a diagram can thus simply string nine "event" beads in a row, with a short description or title for each successive scene unit (Figure 3.2a). This rough-cut plot-bead diagram is already useful, but can and should be refined further to yield more production information.

Drawing a plot-bead diagram is an iterative process. Drawing and re-drawing them is actually a form of thinking. The successive refinements of the diagrams reflect a deepening understanding of the dramatic structure. These re-drawings are, in fact, the *method* for achieving deeper and deeper structural understanding. The fact that we are always working with an *arti-fact* – a "made thing" – is what the drawing process reveals. As an analytical

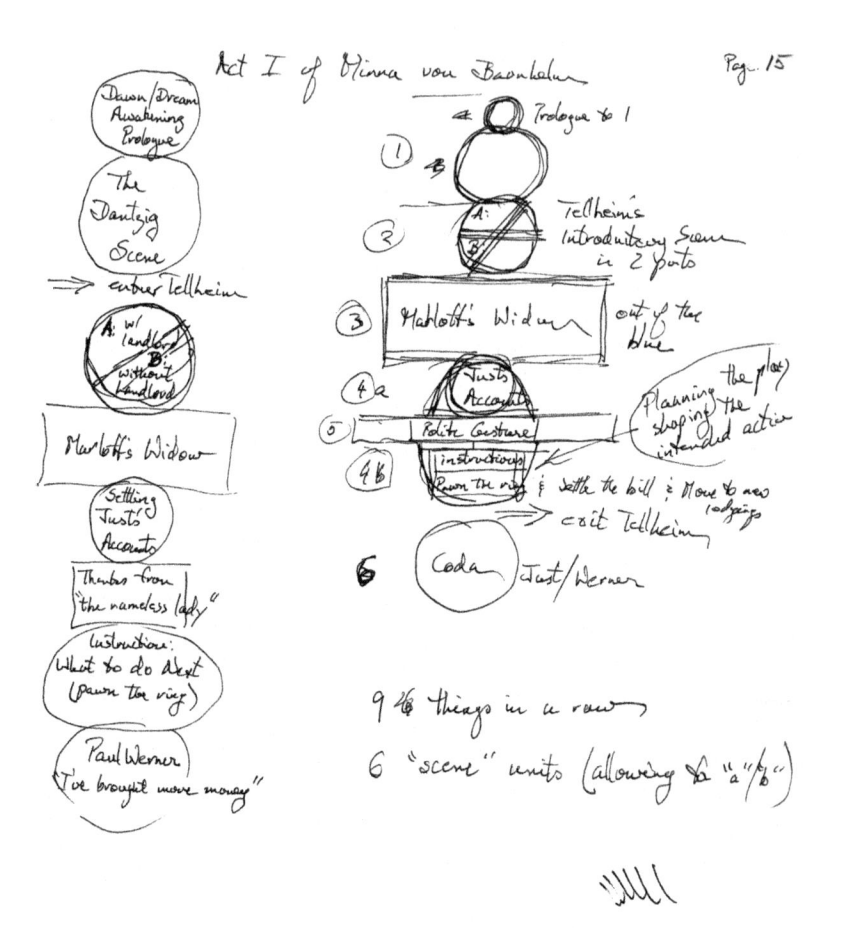

Figure 3.2a Rough-cut plot-bead diagram of Gotthold Lessing's
 Minna von Barnhelm, Act I.

tool, the diagram reveals graphically what we grasp and apprehend as the elusive "time-forms" become clearer and clearer. For playwrights, plot-bead diagrams can also reveal flaws and errors during composition.

As reflected in Figure 3.2b, a more sophisticated analysis reveals that four of the nine "rough beads" are really two divided scenes, each inter-rupted, but each allowed to resume after the interruption, and thus they are single scenes chopped into two halves each. Thus, Act I, on closer inspec-tion, reveals itself to be a five-scene structure. In the more informative (and therefore better) plot-bead diagram (Figure 3.2b), I have labeled the two split scenes 2(a) and 2(b) and 4(a) and 4(b), and that more accurate

Act I of "Minna von Barnhelm"

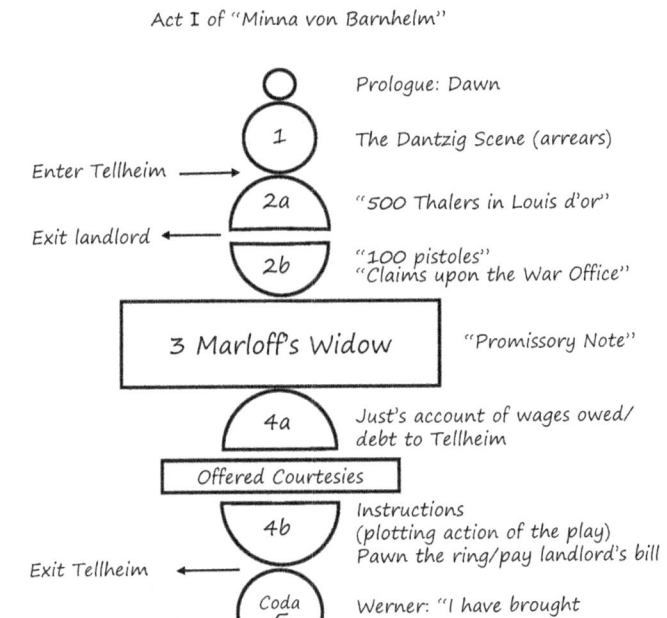

Figure 3.2b More structured plot-bead diagram of Act I of *Minna von Barnhelm*.

structure reveals the deep symmetry of the act – something immediately visible in the diagram. Each of the split scenes (both of them incidentally between Major von Tellheim and his military adjutant, Just – pronounced "Yoost") flanks the central scene of the act. That central scene (scene 3 in the diagram), which I have labeled "Marloff's Widow," is indeed a stand-alone set piece; the central character of this scene appears only here and nowhere else in the play (a casting extravagance greatly discouraged by the economics of contemporary theatre). The symmetrical structure of Act I is really built in both directions from this center. There are, essentially, two scenes leading up to scene 3 – the "Marloff's Widow" scene – and two scenes leading away from it. The two scenes immediately contiguous to the Marloff's Widow scene are "plotting scenes" between Tellheim and Just, and each (as I have already said) is sub-divided into two distinct segments by an interruption. A single scene before and after this cluster – one functioning as the introduction to the act, and the other as the act's coda – rounds out the five-scene "shape" of Act I. Thus, the plot-bead diagram orients us swiftly to the pragmatics of this act, the "things" we have to handle in production: two basic scenes leading into a central stand-alone little drama, and two very similar (and symmetrical) scenes leading us out of the center to the end of the act.

Let us now "read" the plot-bead diagram. The act begins – like many plays in the world repertory – with a dawn prologue. A lone character is revealed in an opening tableau. He is asleep. But his sleep is disturbed by a dream as day breaks. Daybreak is a good starting point in time if one means to respect the notorious "Unity of Time" attributed to Aristotle – and Lessing clearly intended to do so, as we shall see, despite the fact that he was among the Enlightenment scholars who militated against this hard-and-fast classical "rule." Why does it repeatedly occur to dramaturgical craftsmen to follow this rule? I think Goethe stated it best by his explanation that since the drama is played in "real-time" – in a matter of hours (see Chapter 1) – it makes sense for that acting time to be roughly co-terminous with a comparable passage of story time. It is a craft preference, not an imposed aesthetic "rule," but it is illuminating to consider the craftsman/playwright's recurrent pride in adhering to the One Day convention. Whatever his personal motivation might have been, Lessing joined innumerable playwrights, before and after him, in packing the entire action of *Minna von Barnhelm* into a single imaginary day. Thus, the opening "bead" of his prologue already suggests classical play construction – something that already sheds light on ways to understand and handle the play.

The plot continues when the sole character on the stage, fitfully wrestling with his dream, fully awakens. He is then joined by a second character (the minimum required for a classical "scene"), at which point scene 1 properly begins. Note that "scene 1" is thus "event-bead" 2. They are differentiated in the plot-bead diagram in just the same way they need to be differentiated in production: the opening tableau and prologue treated separately as a "unit" preceding the landlord's entrance. I have labeled scene 1 "the Dantzig scene," after its central exchange: the landlord's effort to mollify the angry man who has just awoken – and incidentally, we discover his name at this beginning. The landlord attempts (and comically fails) to pacify his guest by pouring him free drinks – expensive Dantzig liquor. Scene two begins when Major von Tellheim enters (the entrance is the hinge), and the scene that ensues is divided into two halves: the first a squabble with the landlord, and the second a squabble between the Major and his servant (technically, his "batman," a title and position the dramaturg needs to research and explain to the rest of the company) after the landlord has been induced to leave. A brief characterization of both halves of scene 2 might be: dealing with the crisis provoked by the Major's eviction from his room. It proceeds to the point where the Major, increasingly irritated, decides to dismiss his servant.

"Hinges" between beads

Then an interruption (the arrival of Marloff's Widow) stops scene 2 and interposes scene 3, which is played out between the widow and Major Tellheim. Interruptions are basic fare in play construction, and they take many familiar forms: arrivals and departures, knocks at doors and the ringing of doorbells, the piercing jangle of telephone calls, disruptive "noises off," and the like. Sometimes a door simply bursts open and a character intrudes without warning. (Note that that is what the maid's function is in *The Bald Soprano*.) All such plot-division devices are collectively known as *hinges* in a plot. They are basic dramatic punctuation in the ongoing "syntax" of performance events – the ligatures of the formal units. Here the widow's scene serves as a private mini-portrait of the Major's impeccable character: he is seen refusing money owed him, and this despite the financial embarrassment we already know him to be in. The scene is dreadfully sentimental by modern standards, but apparently meant to be taken at face value, as the portrait of a profoundly generous and loyal man – one who displays unswerving devotion to a dead war-companion, pity for a widow and her child, and selfless disregard for his own financial straits.

When the widow leaves (and her scene comes to a natural end, i.e., it runs its course to an unforced exit), Tellheim's man Just returns to continue his interrupted scene with the Major, who had asked him for an account of wages owed him as a preliminary to dismissal from his service. The ensuing scenelet (labeled 4(a) in the diagram) is a continuation and completion of the interrupted scene; it is also in its own right a comic reversal scene – i.e., a scene in which a clearly stated intention (Tellheim's intention to dismiss Just from his service) is thwarted. The device for this reversal is Just's surprising demonstration that far from the Major owing Just, the servant, back wages, it is he, the servant, who is still in debt to his master, and thus he "proves" the impossibility of his being dismissed at this time. This scene follows a traditional and recurrent pattern in comedies – and one Lessing probably studied in Plautus and Molière. It might be labeled "Absurd Reversal via Twisted Logical Proof," and it is still popular as a device in contemporary sitcoms on television. It is capped in this instance by the delightfully emblematic story of the unwanted dog, whose unswerving loyalty cannot be deflected by abuse or neglect. The image is so apt and memorable that one could call the scene, "The Loyal Dog scene."

At this juncture, Just and Tellheim are interrupted by a servant sent by the unknown and unseen lady who has usurped the Major's room. The intruding servant has been asked to offer courtesies to the gentleman who has been forced to cede his lodging. This extended interruption simply hints at developments that will shape the next act, but it is worth pointing out the awkward patching that Lessing resorts to in order to keep story detail from marring his plot plan. The intended development of Lessing's plot will not proceed as planned if Tellheim discovers at this juncture that it is his beloved Minna who happens to have taken up residence in his room. To keep her name from Tellheim, Lessing bends his story frame inside out and backwards to make of this nameless servant (another character who makes a single appearance in a five-act play) a man "who was engaged a few days ago in Dresden" and who has "not heard his mistress's family name yet." Such outlandish improbabilities – clearly forced by plot-necessities – are also a time-honored source of humor in plays: they serve as a wink between author and audience, and acknowledge openly that what we are watching is a constructed play and not at all "Real Life."

When the unnamed and uninformative servant leaves, Tellheim gets down to business and plots the rest of the play: he instructs Just to pawn a valuable ring he has been keeping in his pocket, to pay the outstanding bill with the proceeds, and to take up lodgings elsewhere – preferably in a cheaper place. Scenes like this are everywhere in drama, and they portray the characters in a play actively attempting to shape the plot of the play in which they are appearing. Above, I called this a "plotting scene" for this reason. In comedies, such "best laid plans" are the springboard for comic variation in the way things turn out. In tragedies, such "plotting" by principal characters, whether heroes or villains, usually demonstrates the aching disparity between human intention and the dispositions of fate and chance. Tragedy itself can be defined as the intractable gap in human affairs between intention and outcome. Comedies take this gap for granted as the playing space for *all* comic action. All drama holds our attention by walking this fundamental line between *intended* action and *the way things turn out*. I believe it is one of the eternal fascinations of dramatic representation; what does individual volition propose, and how do the greater "forces" in the world (whatever they might be) in the end dispose? Looked at in this light, plotting scenes can always be treated as far more momentous than they might seem on first reading. Human beings trying to order and control what happens to them are never engaged in something *trivial* (though it may be comic). If plotting scenes are treated in production as no more than tedious mechanical necessities in creaking plot-engines – a frequently dismissive practice of directors who dislike (or misunderstand) the play they have been assigned – they turn out to be as tedious to watch as the reluctant director has assumed they would be *in his own mind*.

Tellheim exits after issuing his instructions, and the act ends with a coda best characterized by one of the first lines spoken by the latest arrival.

No sooner has Tellheim's war-companion (and subordinate officer), Lieutenant Paul Werner, taken the stage, than he delivers the certain laugh line "I have brought some more money!" It puts a finishing cap on a string of nine plot-segments (grouped in my analysis as five basic scenes) that have all, in various ways, centered obsessively around money matters. This amusingly superfluous coda, in fact, points to a pattern that threads through the entire plot-bead diagram: money, money, money, and money again forms the subject of the whole play. Money worries, business opportunities, unpaid bills, debts, accounts receivable, promissory notes, proffered repayments, stashed bags of *louis d'ors*, valuable jewelry, even a bribe of free drinks – these are the incessant concerns of the whole act. No story revelations yet account for such a single-minded obsession with money and exchanges of trade-value. But the plot, looked at closely *as a plot*, already makes this theme a salient identity of Lessing's play. No one can fail to notice it in the plot: this play is all about money. An informed dramaturg will already know that theatre historians class Lessing's play as a decisive example of "bourgeois" comedy, but why might that be, and what does this dominant preoccupation with money imply? What led the author – in this case Gotthold Ephraim Lessing – at a particular time and place, to steep his comedy in this subject matter? Let us leave the plot-beading (which would in practice be continued in similar detail through the remaining four acts of the play) to move ahead to the next stage of the full production process.

Process (4): widening the focus: sources outside the play

Another objective of the production dramaturg is to widen everyone's focus or outlook on the play. Now, after completing the full formal analysis of the play (the complete plot-bead analysis) a process of *lateral* research begins, probing the sources of the play, and the circumstances in Lessing's time (and life) that led to the writing of the play.

Goethe was among the many early admirers of *Minna von Barnhelm*, and one of the reasons he prized the play was that its "source" was contemporary German life at the time of its writing. This in itself was an innovation in German theatre culture, for plays were habitually outsourced in Lessing's time – usually from French and Italian materials. The first production of *Minna von Barnhelm* took place at Hamburg in 1767, but it was not a great success there. It was enthusiastically received, however, in the following year – this time in Prussian Berlin. Lessing himself hinted that the play was essentially finished by 1763, a date that explicitly links the play to the end of the devastating Seven Years' War (1756–1763). No contemporary American director or actor would be likely to know or grasp without guidance the immediate historical implications of a play featuring a recently discharged army officer finding himself disgraced and down and out so soon after his service in Germany's infamous *Siebenjähriger Krieg* – an important watershed in German military history, and one invoked and remembered during every German war since the eighteenth century. Furthermore, the play script contains so few hints about what army Tellheim served in, and against what enemy, that it is virtually impossible for a contemporary English-language reader to deduce from the script alone that Tellheim was a Prussian officer serving Frederick the Great, and that he therefore would have been in active service during the invasion and occupation of Minna von Barnhelm's native Saxony when he met and wooed her. The outrage of Frederick's violent invasion of Saxony was in fact the immediate *cause* of the Seven Years' War, and the war's costs in human bloodshed and economic ruin were near catastrophic. Such details are now remote from us, but they were not lost on Lessing's audience – especially when the play moved to Prussian Berlin during the economic depression that followed the war. These specific postwar and post-defeat aspects of Lessing's play have also been remembered by German audiences whenever the play has been revived in Austria or Germany in the twentieth century. Such context, even when lightly sketched as here, starts mental wheels turning about the meaning and possible interpretation of the play – and that is a major task of research dramaturgy. Plays in public theatres were not normally about current events before Lessing's introduction of this bold example, and the play gave its first audiences a nationalistic jolt of self-recognition that was clearly intentional. *Minna von Barnhelm's* portrait of a neglected military man – a man deeply aggrieved because his character has been maligned – thus has a historical importance and a contemporary significance unrelated to its intrinsic strengths or weaknesses as a play per se. Knowledge of such historical circumstances obviously conditions the way the play is read and received.

A look into Lessing's personal biography lends further suggestion to the contextual matrix of the play. A good dramaturgical reading of the play would by now have isolated the fact that Major von Tellheim is a protagonist *defined* by his unswerving conviction of innocence and his demonstrable financial rectitude. There is no space here for the full biographical survey that a thorough workup would provide, but to illustrate this phase of the process, suffice it to point out that Lessing enjoyed during the war a close friendship with Major Ewald von Kleist, a Prussian military officer who has been identified by German scholars as the model for von Tellheim. Von Kleist was himself a poet who composed a jingoistic celebration in verse, *Ode to the Prussian Army* (*Ode an die preussische Armee*, 1757), at the outset of Frederick's war, after the Prussian monarch ordered his historic pre-emptive invasion of Saxony. During the war, Lessing served as personal secretary to another Prussian officer, the general Tauentzien, stationed at Breslau. This means he was privy to Prussian military thinking in the capital of occupied Silesia, the bone of contention in a previous collision of Frederick's belligerent militaristic state with the Austrian Empire. In short, Lessing was up to his ears in the Prussian military camp, and he had a major stake in normalizing postwar relations between the belligerents who fought and bled each other to exhaustion during the war. The German states were in economic ruin after Frederick's war, and rancours ran deep. Thus, once we catch on to Lessing's evident effort to devise a popular comedy symbolically reconciling Saxon Germans to their recent Prussian oppressors, the Minna–Tellheim alliance takes on a charged theatrical valence. One final detail, by way of example of how biographical research can broaden one's "take" on a play, concerns an incident in Lessing's life that precedes the writing of the play by two decades. While still a student, in the 1740s, Lessing had been forced to flee the city of Leipzig to avoid arrest for debt. Literary scholars tell us to avoid conjecturing interpretatively from such biographical data, but it is legitimate to feed an actor's or a director's imagination with such biographical correlations. Who can tell how scared and humiliated the young Lessing might have felt, but his plight helps us comprehend the almost pathological degree to which Tellheim identifies his personal honor with strict fiscal rectitude. These tissues of context all lend imaginative potency to the play and to its many invented details. Enriched context should serve as inspiration for the director, the designers, and eventually the actors in the major roles. In practice, the collective suggestive power of contextual facts and detail is the whole purpose of research dramaturgy. It *supplements* the play because such research is done outside of the immediate formal bounds of the playscript.

We now have a very different picture of what *Minna von Barnhelm* is "about." At a deeper level than the frothy details of a comic eviction from an inn, unpaid bills, and estranged lovers, the play is "about" what might be called the Frederick material: Prussian militarism, nationalistic ambition and war guilt and reparation. The pathology of soldiers returning to civilian life, where they confront the friction between their own battle-tested sense of personal worth (their conviction of superiority), and the petty bourgeois ethics and concerns of peacetime civilians toiling to turn a profit. Much of the play centers on the dogged equation of all "value" with money, financial rectitude, and a good credit rating. What Karl Marx within two generations of the first performance of this play (1767) would be calling "the commodification of all value" and "the reification of money," Lessing presented as the groundwork for the principal *action* of his contemporary "bourgeois" comedy.

Looked at in this light, *Minna von Barnhelm* has a fascination it lacks as a face-value comedy. It suggests why it has a greater cultural value in Germany and Austria than it has ever achieved in England or America. It also suggests a surprising correlation of this neglected play (largely eclipsed from American consciousness) to the Wilson/Müller work – *the CIVIL warS*, mentioned above – that won (but was denied) the anomalous Pulitzer Prize in 1986. We now are in a better position to understand the contributions to that project of the East German playwright Heiner Müller, who wrote and assembled original texts on "the Frederick material" that revisited dramaturgical ground very similar to that which we have uncovered behind *Minna von Barnhelm*. Included among the original texts he wrote and collated at Robert Wilson's invitation for Act IV of *the CIVIL warS*, are Müller's own dark broodings about Frederick the (so-called) Great, side by side with historical letters and journal entries by the real Frederick and his father. Müller also spliced in passages from the writings of Karl Marx on money, and other politically charged materials that cover the same dramaturgical matrix we have just unearthed for *Minna von Barnhelm*. Müller can be seen to have been exploring the colossal contradictions between personal rectitude and military tyranny, between intellectual Enlightenment and battlefield atrocities, between the delicate refinements of baroque flute-playing and the slaughter and rapine of all-out modern warfare. We are meant to remember that when he rose to power, Hitler placed a wreath at Frederick's tomb, and when he committed suicide, he did so apparently standing before Frederick's portrait. Robert Wilson added a provocative sub-title to *the CIVIL warS: a tree is best measured when it is down.*

That phrase, strangely enough, characterizes *Minna von Barnhelm* very well, for Major von Tellheim has been placed (by Lessing, the playwright) into his predicament precisely because his *character* is "best measured when he is down." Lessing's play is a portrait of a neglected military hero, an impeccably "good" man (by strictly bourgeois standards) who is nurturing in secret his own outraged sense of slighted virtue; von Tellheim is seen simmering at a slow boil: he quietly *cultivates* his conviction of superiority through active *self-denial*, a sort of stoic pouting that refuses anything that would help him out of his distress – even that which is due to him – for to accept *any remedy* short of full vindication would undercut his position as a victim of injustice. Tellheim eventually equates his sense of personal honor with his victimization: were his affliction to end, his identity as a wounded superior being would be disrupted. This portrait of wounded pride is reinforced theatrically by the injured arm Lessing has thrown in for good measure, a major pathetic stage "effect" never absent in performance, but one easily overlooked in a narrow *literary* overview that fails to visualize a performance. With all our dramaturgical ducks in a row, we would make sure no one tried to play Tellheim without featuring the crippled arm.

None of the enriching materials here presented come up spontaneously from even seven readings of *Minna von Barnhelm*. Without a great deal of research, thought, and analysis, these dimensions of what is otherwise a very frothy and conventional comedy could easily be missed. After full immersion in the enriched *context* surrounding the play and its composition, the focused discipline of the plot-bead diagram takes us back to the specific mechanisms of the comedy, its verve and its pace, its clever individual "routines" and its essential romantic core, but the *full* dramaturgical workup gives a production team additional potentialities to work with in planning a revival of the play. How might it be handled *this time*? Do we just play the comedy for speed and for fun (the usual "take" on most comedies)? What might we do in production with suggestions about the play's role in the German consciousness, with these manifest links in the play to the recurrent rise of aggrieved and self-righteous militarism after cycles of humiliation and defeat? How does the wound of the Vietnam debacle in America, for instance, or the various Gulf wars illuminate the play? Is there a worthwhile link that might be explored through production decisions? We are now launched on the sort of production planning that should precede every good production, but imagine having already committed to first impressions that never considered any of the deeper dramaturgical potency invested in the play.

Process (5): the "take" on the play: what will it be this time?

Next, the production process is poised for a decision: how will the play be treated *this time*? In theatre practice, it is the director's prerogative to determine the "take" on the play. This decision should be taken in the light of all available analytical and research materials, as outlined above. Many directors ask their production dramaturg for a comprehensive production history (step II, 3 of the Full Dramaturgical Workup) to guide their thinking as they home in on "the take this time." Such directors are acutely conscious of their work and its place in an ongoing evolution of the art of the stage. For this reason, they want to know traditional ways the play has been taken, interpreted, and presented. They also want to place their own upcoming production in an ongoing dialogue, which requires that they be up-to-date on recent values discovered or brought forth by their fellow artists, and the critical debate these productions sparked – wherever they may have been presented. In Europe, such dialogue among major directors amounts almost to a rivalry analogous to the competition between regional sports teams. What has Peter Brook done in Paris, or Peter Stein in Germany, or Luca Ronconi or Giorgio Strehler in Milan and Rome? Has Ingmar Bergman somewhere done a version of the play? Did Ariane Mnouchkine do a version in her Théâtre du Soleil? What of Peter Hall, or Declan Donnellan, or Deborah Warner in London? And what major actors have interpreted the principal roles? What was their "take" on the play? How was it received? What designers worked on each production, and what visual style dominated their work? Are there photo archives of this work? Did Robert Wilson do a version anywhere? Christoph Marthaler in Hamburg or Zurich? François Rochaix in Paris or Geneva? Andrei Serban in Belgrade or London? Krystian Lupa in Kraków? A comprehensive production history will put answers to such questions at the disposal of the production team.

The production history stems from the recognition that each individual production of a play is *one version* of an endlessly mutable artistic and cultural "object." This aspect of play production, and the seemingly complex *identity* of all art objects that are performance events, has drawn a tremendous amount of abstruse critical and theoretical attention in the past 30 years. But the issue is also a very accessible practical one, and it has straightforward common-sense parameters. In practice, there is good sense in a blunt question like "are we going to be doing it straight, or are we giving it a spin?" These are not very precise terms perhaps, but they get at the heart of the matter in real situations. There are two poles of directorial orientation implied by the practical question posed above, and a quick shorthand for the issue contrasts the "transparent" (or faithful) director to the auteur–director, who takes compositional liberties.

The transparent director sees his job as featuring the *play* – on its own terms – in the best light possible. When his work is done, the transparent director "disappears," leaving no trace but the perfectly realized play – with all credit and attention directed toward the actors and to the playwright. Transparent directors supposedly aim at an ideally "definitive" production, which does full justice to the essential genius of the play. This ideal is (I hasten to add) an abstraction, and it infringes on the controversial notion of "author's intent," which is currently out of fashion. But the ideal of transparent directing is founded on a stark fact that is hard to refute: modern life is such that no actor or director usually engages any given play more that once (or at most twice) in an artistic lifetime. The actor doing his fifth *Hamlet*, for instance, is an anomaly. And for audience members, the chances are similarly remote that they will see many productions of any one play in a lifetime of theatre-going. Each production is therefore an extremely important event in the life of everyone concerned: actors, audience, director, designers, and the theatre itself, if it is an institution that is compiling a self-conscious history. The "take" on any one play will have very wide cultural consequences; it should therefore not be determined (so the argument goes) by whimsy, or a careless, accidental, or impetuous set of choices. The transparent director acknowledges an inherent cultural "right" nested in the artifact we call a play. It is his or her duty to respect and live up to that artifact's inherent qualities. Genius, in this view, resides in the *form* of the play.

The so-called auteur–director is an abstraction at the other end of an imaginary aesthetic spectrum that runs from complete fidelity to "author's intent" at one extreme, to complete usurpation of the prerogatives of the artist/playwright at the other. Auteur–directors are expected to take the bit between their teeth and to astonish us with their own invention and originality. Play scripts are starting points for their own original composition in the theatre, and auteur–directors recognize no *a priori* "rights" of either the play, its themes, or its author: if an auteur–director feels compelled to change something, he or she will change it. They may do this seriously or whimsically: their *freedom* is the paramount value, not some sacred and static aspect of a play script, like its form, its content, its intended effect, or its supposed cultural importance. Auteur–directors are notorious iconoclasts when it comes to re-interpreting the "classics." But they can just as easily depart from a new and unknown script – inventing, embroidering, and taking liberties as the work progresses. Many untried new scripts are immeasurably enhanced by powerful auteur–directors, who can make *anything* intensely theatrical. The epitomizing fantasy about the ideal auteur–director is that she can be handed a telephone book, and make compelling theatre out of it.

Forced to generalize, one might naturally argue that in such a public art as the theatre, each individual production carries a *cultural* responsibility that should be met consciously, and furthermore that that responsibility can only be met with depths of professional discipline and focused artistry. Either type of director can be represented as satisfying such a deep cultural responsibility – the "transparent" director transmitting a culture that would be lost without him, the auteur–director creating and renewing a culture which would ossify and die without her. Copyright *legislates* this responsibility, and that legal intrusion into art is often resented by artists who feel constrained by the force of restrictive laws impinging on their work. By the same token, the "transparent" ideal of a morally imposed cultural responsibility *invites* a spirit of rebellion, transgression, and renewal. Escaping legal constraints by choosing a play outside the "copyright shadow" (discussed further below) very naturally appeals to ambitious stage directors. And some flamboyant directors have been attracted to the controversial practice of flouting copyright restrictions, thus provoking a legal showdown over their artistic freedom. "Fresh" can come to mean, in such deliberately contentious situations, free of *any* imposed responsibility. Much can be said and debated about the range of acceptable latitude in play production. Suffice it here to say, in this overview of process and the role of Production Dramaturgy, that the dramaturgical ideal is to make no *uninformed* decisions about the handling of any specific play in production. The fundamental idea is to be in a position to compare the original context and motivation for *writing the play* to the present context and motivation for *mounting this production*.

Process (6): the acting edition

Any decision about the specific handling of a play in a particular production will be reflected in the selection and preparation of the acting edition – the script actually placed in the hands of the actors, and taken as our central tool into the rehearsal hall. Whenever a play goes into production, the director and the literary staff (or the front office) select the acting edition. When there are several choices (e.g., a foreign play available in competing translations) it is the production dramaturg's job to assist the director in selecting and preparing the company's acting edition before it is distributed to the designers and the actors. Most of the time, script selection is governed by contract law: a specific copyrighted text is available for what amounts to a leasing arrangement between the playwright's agent and the producing theatre. In these typical cases, the law requires that no changes be made to the script without explicit (usually written) permission from the author or his/her agent, and copyright law is fairly closely adhered to in American theatre practice. These legal strictures, while widely accepted, do impinge on the artistic freedom of performers and their directors, and there is an inherent *structural* conflict between these explicit author's rights and the creative latitude of directors and actors. De facto negotiations take place every day across this legal boundary. It is the production dramaturg's business to be highly sensitive to both sides of this structural conflict. In practice, dramaturgs are frequently expected to function as advocates for missing playwrights, and in this role, they are expected to defend the playwright's "right" to have his composition presented without distortion. To do so, the dramaturg needs to have a working understanding of the "intent" of the script, as well as a good practical knowledge of the basic requirements of copyright law. But dramaturgs are also team players in an evolving production, and the creative dynamic of the rehearsal hall must also be respected. All plays are continually improved by discoveries in the rehearsal hall; such innovation is the life blood of dramatic art, and no script can be thought of as *completed* until it has been produced and acted before an audience. All this is pretty clear during the evolution of a new play, but problems crop up once established plays go beyond their initial production. Dramaturgy can and should contribute to the debate *before* decisions are made.

Once a play is selected, the director and the dramaturg prepare the acting edition. On the simplest level, this means looking up all the meanings (and pronunciations) of difficult words, or the definitions of technical terms, or the exact connotation of ranks, relationships, and titles.

Artistic freedom and the "copyright shadow"

The available plays for production divide into two groups: those protected by copyright and those outside such protection. All contemporary plays are protected by copyright, and what might be called the "shadow" of that protection extends backwards into the past (in the U.S., potentially as far back as 1923, if the original copyright was renewed). To call the zone of protection a "shadow" is to take the typical producer's and director's point of view, for dramatic authors consider the *un*protected sphere the "shadow" zone. What is at stake is the obligation to pay a fee and – the more important issue for most artists – legal control of the nature and form of the play. Copyright, in effect, is seen either as a curb or a guarantee of "artistic freedom," depending on whose role one favors in the theatre equation. For directors determined to gain maximum artistic elbow-room, there is a theoretically vast "unprotected" repertory of plays spanning two-and-a-half millennia. But even this theoretically limitless availability of plays from the history of the theatre is infringed by the copyrights of modern translations and adaptations, which are as valid and as restrictive (and also require the payment of fees for use) as are the copyrights of recently composed plays. Ever-renewed translations are needed to keep most classics alive and viable in the contemporary performance repertory. Thus the huge creative latitude the historical repertory represents for directors is hemmed in by the legal rights of translators and adaptors. Production Dramaturgy must mediate between the limitless creative freedom almost all directors wish for, and the curtailing "rights" of authors and their translators. For all these reasons, many theatres find it both cheaper and more expedient to commission "original" translations and adaptations of the classics for individual productions at that theatre. The ideal person for those adaptations and translations is the theatre's own resident dramaturg, if he or she has the competency to accomplish the task. But a market has cropped up for skilled translator/adaptors, and they bring their commissioned work essentially as new plays to the producing theatre, frequently teamed with directors with whom they have learned to collaborate smoothly and efficiently (examples of such teams are Shelley Berc and Andrei Belgrader; Robert Auletta and François Rochaix; James Magruder and Irene Lewis).

Process (7): rehearsal work: action analysis

As a production moves from planning stages into the rehearsal hall, the dramaturgical focus shifts to action analysis, the specific province of actors and their director. Central as it is to dramaturgy, the detailed isolation and identification of *character* actions in a play – moment to moment, character by character, beat by beat, scene by scene, act by act – is not specifically the production dramaturg's business. But discerning "The Action" of any portion of a dramatic artifact is a crucial skill at the heart of dramaturgy. Plot-bead analysis sub-divides the whole of a play into a string of parts; it gives us an indispensable *formal overview*, and it lays open the play to the nitty-gritty of individual rehearsals. From the high vantage of an overview of the *totality* of the play-structure, we descend in rehearsal to the close-up assessment of the "genius of each scene." There is no formal unit – from each individual phoneme to the overall architecture of the whole performance event – to which action analysis does not apply. As the dramaturg learns to encompass larger and larger conceptual units, it gradually becomes second nature to flair out "The Action" of each scene (which includes all the individual actions of the many characters *in* the scene), and beyond these to apprehend "The Action" of each act, and ultimately "The Action" of the whole play. This dramaturgical shift in focus and scale is predicated on the assumption that composers (in this case playwrights) work from deep aesthetic core principles (their style or "genius") and that dramaturgs are there to *read* this core aesthetic: they must get in tune with the action of *making* the play.

These twin actions – the character's and the playwright's – are easy to confuse, so much so that many neophyte playwrights hopelessly intermix their own *composing* action with the supposed actions of their characters. It is important to learn to differentiate between character action (what Aristotle called *praxis*) and the artistic action of the composer of the scene (what the Greeks called *poiesis*). All manipulations of scene form (including the writing of lines) are done for a *purpose*. This is craft, or *poiesis*. Simultaneously, all character actions within a scene (including the lines they "speak") attempt to accomplish a character-purpose. This is action, or *praxis*. Aristotelian dramatic theory suggests that, in a successful play, the two actions converge in a unity of achievement. In other words, the playwright's aesthetic action *contains* the individual actions of the represented characters. When conducting an action analysis (to find *the action* of a scene, for instance) it is important to be able to tell the characters' purposes from those of their playwright. Lessing may make Tellheim refuse the widow's money "to demonstrate his impeccable character," but is that Tellheim's *action* in that same scene? What's driving *him* is quite distinct from what drove Lessing to write the scene.

The dramaturg's analytical work during a rehearsal thus differs from the actor's character-centered "motive hunting." In both cases, however, we are talking about the fine art of tuning one's histrionic sensibility to a governing aesthetic. The actor finds his or her focus in *what the character is presented as doing*, and the production dramaturg tries to track *what the playwright/composer was doing* in arranging the incidents into a particular plot. At the level of immediate attention that characterizes rehearsal work – i.e., *this* moment of the play, these characters, in this exact situation, doing and saying *this* – Stanislavski technique is still central, and most directors at work in America derive their rehearsal technique from that one source, via many channels of transmission. Dramaturgs can usefully think of themselves as *custodians of the formal cause*, in parallel with actors who live out, on a different conceptual track, the imagined lives of the characters within the play. The dramaturg remains outside looking in, assessing the whole, while the actors insinuate themselves inside the fiction to play out the implications of the score.

What the production dramaturg should be tracking and mastering *in parallel* with ongoing rehearsal work, is the overall action *of the play*, or its master through-line – its "spine" in Stanislavski parlance. There are many books one can consult for this level of action-lore and training techniques for getting better at discerning and identifying actions. *A Practical Handbook for the Actor*, by Scott Zigler et al., is one of the ones I recommend because it is sound in its technique, efficiently brief, and it yields quick and reliable practical results (Bruder et al., 1986).

Process (8): disseminating dramaturgical information

Once the rehearsal process begins, much wider dissemination of appropriate dramaturgical materials is needed, extending to the publicity department, the development office, the box office, patrons, and school groups. I mention this here in the interest of being thorough, so that no part of a production dramaturg's full job description goes unrecorded here. Production dramaturgs are typically engaged during the rehearsal period providing "enrichment" packets to those in rehearsal, essays for newsletters, press release material in preparation for interviews with the production's artists, dramaturgical pages for the playbill, and study guides suitable for various education levels. These assignments also prepare the production dramaturg for supplemental lectures and symposium presentations, pre-show discussions and "talk-backs."

The resident dramaturg's interface with a wider public is (ideally) built around a principle closer to art appreciation than to marketing. Dramaturgy can go a long way in getting audiences up to speed for their experience in the theatre, especially in mediating the new and unfamiliar. In this important way, resident dramaturgs build a theatre's audience base. To introduce and promote an aesthetic, one must thoroughly understand it; and nothing more thoroughly tests one's understanding of an aesthetic than trying to write or speak about it. Enhancing the public's enjoyment of a live performance is in itself a "dramaturgical" principle that should be made explicit in a company dramaturg's job description.

Process (9): Production Dramaturgy in tech and previews

After a play in production leaves the rehearsal hall, it enters a period of instability that is known as "production week" or "tech" in most theatres. Many bad things can happen during production week, but many of these bad things can be mitigated by careful planning and good dramaturgical methodology through this crucial transition period. The play as it has been rehearsed tends, temporarily, to fall apart. Attention is scattered, concentration is impossible, continuity cannot be achieved, and all the discoveries of the rehearsal process tend to cool in the mind, to recede from memory, to become less present. Everyone gets the impression that the precious rehearsal discoveries are slipping away. Simultaneously, since opening night is rapidly approaching, and full public exposure is just days away, anxiety and anticipation rise, everyone gets nervous, and the flush and adrenaline of performance start to manifest themselves in tempers and nerves. Typically, a producer or artistic director (whose authority can override both the director and the stage manager) shows up at this stage, and unless *that* person is experienced and sage, premature judgments, impatience, and disapproval (based on observed chaos) can and all-too frequently do apply destructive stress and sow distraction and diffidence among the artists at work. The whole mix is inexpressibly volatile, and only thorough preparation, strong professional discipline, and full competency in the stage management staff can keep a production from flying apart at this stage. Production dramaturgs should keep a very low profile during tech. They should, above all, never give actors notes or advice. But they should observe keenly, and *take notes*.

Contemporary theatre practice in America has incorporated the "preview" week into full production schedules (and budgets). Previews cost money because actors continue to rehearse and directors continue to direct in this interim. Production dramaturgs also have a role to play during preview, and this role differs from the support roles enumerated above at all the other stages of the process. The idea of an "in-house critic" has been at the root of dramaturgy from its inception. Lessing, arguably the first official "dramaturg" in the European tradition, was hired as an "in-house critic." He alienated his sponsors and the Hamburg acting company by excessive honesty. The term "in-house critic" has misled generations of dramaturgs, and it should not be taken as an accurate job description at all – except during previews. The production dramaturg can at this stage (and only at this stage) usefully role-play the "outside" critic, and anticipate the point of view of a reviewer – sharing judiciously plausible critical reactions with the director. It should be emphatically stressed that such opinions and criticisms should be shared *with the director alone*. A great deal of mischief can be done to a production when a meddlesome or gossipy production dramaturg starts a grape-vine undercurrent of criticism and carping misgivings. But an experienced director can benefit enormously from shared hints about plausible critical response from a trusted member of his team. The key to ongoing process is that during previews something can still be done about perceived flaws and weaknesses. But the relationship of criticism to the energies of creation and performance is a delicate one: confidence is an essential ingredient in strong performance. Consequently, great care, tact, and judgment need to go into these final dramaturgical exchanges between production dramaturgs and directors, for the director's final "brush-up" instructions to his actors are a crucial test of that director's control over the production. Notes taken in silence and given *in writing* to the director (who may then use them as he or she sees fit, at a time of his or her choosing) are usually the best way to communicate preview insights and opinions.

Process (10): the long run: archiving production materials

Once the play opens, the production dramaturg's work is essentially done. Production dramaturgs – especially if they are resident in the theatre – have a few follow-up duties to attend to, in order to fully wrap up the production. Chief among these is archiving the production. All the production's dramaturgical materials are potentially valuable, and should be archived. This means not only preserving the materials, but also organizing them in such a way that they are accessible and useful in the future. The likely future audience for these materials are fellow dramaturgs about to launch another production of the play, or scholars, theatre historians, and biographers seeking "eyewitness" documentation of the production and the work of the artists associated with it.

Making a difference

The public and the critics who attend plays hold theatres accountable for their experience in the public "seeing place," and the tendency of those on the dark side of the footlights is conservative. "We want our classics treated with respect." So pronounced is this cultural inertia, that a reverse "obligation to provoke" often occurs to the artists on the hot side of the footlights. Dramaturgs ideally mediate at this interface, and a living theatre maintains a balance between innovation and tradition, between expanding consciousness and the deep cultural moorings of tradition and historical continuity.

Stanislavski, who was (as is everyone) steeped in the aesthetics of his era, used to talk of the "germ" or "kernel" of a play, and by that he apparently meant the inner inspiration that organized all an author's energies around the creation of a work of art. The underlying assumption behind an idea such as "the integrity of art forms" is that all manmade artifacts (including plays) embody authorial purposes. A playwright's intentions are deeply enmeshed in the conventions of the stage as they were established when the play was composed. Imagination is projected *into* something. Good Production Dramaturgy can make it its business to discern and recover a work's genetic spark. Our dramaturgical purpose in collecting collateral information about a play and its circumstances of composition is to understand its performance dynamic: to recover the way it organizes and activates creative energy when staged and played.

Every production is a new interaction with a constructed artifact, and the result is invariably yet another artifact that is a variation on the basic idea at the core of each play. Discerning a play's germ or kernel (a poietic motive) is a precious idea, and so is the idea of its faithful cultural transmission. A production dramaturg trained to believe a play's "germ" is recoverable, will certainly unearth something transportable from place to place and from time to time.

The conservative implications of curatorial dramaturgy operate side by side with a countervailing obligation to renew the art form. Both obligations can lay claim to the phrase "conscience of the theatre." The case needs to be made for lifting the dramaturgical mind and imagination out of excessive respect and fidelity to the past and re-centering it in the here-and-now of immediate production where the felt obligation is to the contemporary audience, and to the culture at large and its present crises. The theatre as an art form has a long history of questioning the past, of disrupting common expectations, of using transgressive performance as a social safety valve, of thumbing its nose at tradition, and challenging the status quo. There is an obligation to have fun and make fun in the theatre, and to remember that a spirit of escape, of holiday revel, of delight, discovery, and astonishment are expected and due. In all situations that are not premieres, plays come to us from some cultural locus in the past, but they are also (and invariably) about to become a new object in the present.

References

Bruder, M., Cohn, L.M., Olnek, M., Pollack, N., Previtio, R., Zigler, S., and Mamet, D. (1986) *A Practical Handbook for the Actor.* New York: Random House

Esslin, M. (1961) *The Theatre of the Absurd.* New York: Anchor Books.

Lessing, G. (1972) *Minna von Barnhelm.* Translated by K.J. Northcott. Chicago: University of Chicago Press. (Originally published 1767.)

Afterword
Some closing thoughts for playwrights

> An artist afraid to do it badly is already failing as an artist.
>
> (Heather McHugh (paraphrased, from *Not a Prayer*))
>
> Is there any material art or artisanship that is undercut by a progressive understanding of how to make the thing?
>
> (Elaine Scarry (from *Dreaming by the Book*))

Dramaturgy as presented in this book is a discipline practiced professionally in theatre companies during the production of plays. Its applications to the specifics of playwriting deserve a separate book, but in this brief Afterword I note a few suggestive ways in which the principles – indispensable for the *analysis* of already-written plays – can by anticipation guide the difficult art of composing play scripts, especially for beginners.

A would-be playwright who starts by writing dialogue is starting at the opposite end of a creative and imaginative process that must be based not in what people say but in what they attempt to *do*, the spine of the plot. To build a full-length dramatic *plot* requires an effort of the imagination that I can best express as the mental equivalent of "palming" a medicine ball. Everyone knows what an advantage it is when playing basketball to be physically large: not only to be near the basket, but to handle and control the ball. To compose a *play*, a playwright must "hold" in her mind a clear guiding image of an envisioned *action*, whole and complete, about to unfold itself in time – and this is what a plot-bead diagram achieves. It thus makes sense to envision a full anticipatory plot diagram as a guide for "filling in" the scenes of a new play. This used to be called preparing a scene-by-scene *scenario* before writing dialogue.

To frame the mind to the work of composition for the stage, one must incite the imagination to *anticipate* the stage event. This effort of imagination is at its hardest when the inner core of the dramatic plot is not yet constructed in the mind. Playwrights are doing their particular *poietic* work when they are clarifying, in their minds, an intended *structure of action*. When one is striving to write a play, one must fill the empty page with what Elaine Scarry in her book on aesthetics, *Dreaming by the Book* (2001), calls "delayed sensory content" – instructions for some future reconstruction of a real and immediate performance.

For conceptual clarity, scene writing and plot building – making the parts and arranging them into a whole – are frequently discussed procedurally, as though one activity necessarily preceded the other: that scenes must be written before they can be arranged into larger structures, or that a master plan must precede the methodical "filling in" of the parts. In practice it is likely that the two will be highly interactive, with constant shifting back and forth from one activity to the other. Scenes are written, then arranged into a plot; plot developments are planned, then scenes are written according to that plan – and re-written – and re-arranged – and so on.

The plot-bead diagram and the habit of "plot-beading" can help with this. The aim for playwrights is to develop an acutely conscious grasp of the relation between individual segments of a play (what Chapter 1 teaches us to draw as "beads" in a plot-bead diagram) and the completed structural whole that makes the artifact "One Play." "The Plot" should be the result of the *artful* concatenation of all the individual time-segments we have called "beads."

These remarks are necessarily just hints in this short space. But they imply a direction for a serious apprenticeship: take seriously the formal idea that a coherent play imitates one action. This has little to do with "telling a story." Constructing a play is a poietic craft based on successive *created* time-durations. Design these consciously according to principles. Plan these as a meaningful sequence, and fill them in as actions. None of this is easy or obvious, but technique matters, and sound technique teaches as it proceeds. It is necessary, to be a playwright, to "activate" vivid fictions in the mind until they move and/or talk, but a vigilant poet (the playwright) needs always to control *form* once the fictions start to move. To do that, you have to know what an action is *as a term of art*.

Reference

Scarry, E. (2001). *Dreaming by the Book.* Princeton, NJ: Princeton University Press.

Index

Page numbers in *italics* denote figures.

action 9, x, xi, xv, 5, 49–70; anatomy
    of an action 55, 56–59; of the author
    64–65; complete actions 53–55;
    finding an 59–61; in full
    dramaturgical workup 76; human
    "doings" 6–8, 63; language as
    symbolic/Burke's legacy 69–70;
    linking to form 47–48; overview
    6–8; rehearsal work/action analysis
    102–103; spheres of action/theatres
    65–69, *67*; Stanislavski's legacy
    61–63; structure of 108–109; as a
    term of art 49–53
action beats 26
action painting xiv
actors 6–8, 10, 24, 60–61; rehearsal
    work 102–103; *see also* playscripts:
    acting edition; Stanislavski System
acts 25–26, 52
adaptations 8, 101
Aeschylus xiii; *Oresteia* xv, 67
agency 52
American Laboratory Theatre 49
American Repertory Theatre (A.R.T.)
    5, 40, 79, 80
analysis *see* plot-bead diagrams
analytical/critical thinking 9–11
archiving production materials 105
Aristophanes, *Thesmophoriazusae* xiii
Aristotle x, xv, 3, 18, 25, 42, 55;
    anatomy of an action 55, 56–59;
    complete action 54, 55, 65; praxis 9,
    5, 47, 49–51, 55, 65, 102; *Peri
    Psyches* (*De Anima*) 55, 58, 61; *The*

Poetics 5, 17, 21–22, 47–48, 49–51,
    54, 55
Arrabal, Fernando xii
artistic freedom 6, 99–102
Augustine, Saint, *Confessions* 18, 19,
    22
Auletta, Robert 102
authors *see* playwrights
avant-garde xi–xiii, 36, 86

backstory 75, 80–87
Beaumarchais, Pierre xii–xiii
Beckett, Samuel xii, 40, 86; *Breath* 22;
    Endgame xv; *Rough for Theatre II* 4,
    41–47, *42*
beginnings 22–24
Belgrader, Andrei 102
Berc, Shelley 102
Bergman, Ingmar 98
Bogart, Anne xiv
Boleslavsky, Richard 49
bouleusis 56–57
boulevard xiii
Brecht, Bertolt 86
Breuer, Lee xiv; *Red Horse Animation*
    xv; *Shaggy Dog Animation* xiii
Brook, Peter 98
Brustein, Robert 5
Burke, Kenneth 49, 51–52; legacy
    69–70; *A Grammar of Motives* 52
Byrd Hoffman School of Byrds xii

Café La Mama E.T.C. xii
causation 60

cause: efficient 63; formal 24, 62, 103;
material 64
Chaikin, Joseph xii
character xi, 7, 59, 60, 62, 96, 102–103
Chekhov, Anton 62
Childs, Lucinda 37
codas 32–34, 41, 45–46, 58
collaboration 11
Comédie Française xii
Commedia dell'arte xiii
content 16–17
context 76, 86, 93–97
conventions xii, 69
copyright 99–102
core of a play 75, 78, 106
Corneille, Pierre xii
crisis in action 54
cubism xiv
cultural responsibility 99–100
cuts 76

dance x, 61
Dante Alighieri 50; *moto spiritale* 55,
65; *Purgatorio* 18
de Kooning, Willem xiv
de Man, Paul 7
Derrida, Jacques 7
Descartes, René 65–66
Dewey, John, *Art as Experience* 51
dialogue 19, 26–27, 79–80, 108; its
relation to action 47, 52, 60, 69–70
dianoia 56
directors x, 2–3, 61; auteur-directors
64, 99; during production process 78,
98, 105; structural conflicts of 9–12
Donnellan, Declan 98
drama ix–x; as term 6
dramatism 51–52
dramatourgos, as term 2
Dramaturgical Moment 74
dramaturg 1–2, 72–74, 101; as custodian
of form 24, 40, 103; as playwright's
advocate 12, 100, 103, 106; as
in-house critic 2, 79, 105; relationship
with director 9–12, 105; *see also*
dramaturgy; production dramaturgy
dramaturgy 1–12; basic principles of
x–xii, 3–8, *4*; applying the principles
of 8–9; as term 2, 72; *see also* action;
form; production dramaturgy

duration 3, 14, 17, 19–25, 27, 36; unit
of duration 3, 19–20, 25, 45

editing, text 76
Eliot, T.S. x
endings 22–24; *see also* codas
episodes, as term 26
essay writing 74
Esslin, Martin 84
Euripides xiii; *Alcestis* 40
experience 51, 81
exposition 81, 84, 86

Feydeau, Georges, *Occupe-toi d'Amélie*
xiii
Fergusson, Francis 49–50, 55, 65, 79
fictional actions xi, xiii–xiv, 6–7, 53,
64–65, 103, 109
film 27–28
Foreman, Richard xii–xiii, xiv, 4;
Pandering to the Masses xiii
form 9, x, 3–6, 13–48, 84; beginnings
and endings 22–24; and content
confusions 14–17, *15*, *16*; linking to
action 47–48; and production process
79; in the theatre 13–14; "formal
cause" 24, 62, 103; *see also* time;
duration; plot-bead diagrams; unity,
aesthetic
formalism 13
Foucault, Michel 37
freedom *see* artistic freedom
French scenes 26
Fyfe, W. Hamilton 50–51

Genet, Jean xii
Gehry, Frank xii
gist 75, 80–84
Glass, Philip 36, 39
Goethe, Johann Wolfgang von xiii, 90,
93
Goldoni, Carlo xiii
Gorki, Maxim 62
Graham, Martha x
Greenberg, Clement xiv

Hall, Peter 98
Harvard University, Institute for
Advanced Theatre Training 9, 11, 83
histrionic sensibility 60, 76, 79, 103

Hornby, Richard, *The End of Acting* 61
Hugo, Victor xii; xiii

Ibsen, Henrik xiii, 81–82; *Ghosts* 82;
   When We Dead Awaken 4, 25,
   40–41; *The Wild Duck* 82
Ionesco, Eugène xii; *The Bald Soprano*
   46, 84–87, *85*, 91
Impressionists xiv, 65

Jarry, Alfred, *Ubu Roi* xiii

Kleist, Ewald Christian von 94

Laclos, Pierre Cholderlos de, *Les
   Liaisons Dangeureuses* 40
La Fontaine, Jean de xii
Lamartine, Alphonse de xii
language as symbolic action 69–70
law 66–67
LeCompte, Elizabeth xiv
Lehmann, Hans Thies xi; xiii
Lessing, Gotthold Ephraim 19;
   Hamburgische Dramaturgie 2;
   Laocoön 3, 14, 22; *Minna von
   Barnhelm* 80–84, 86, 87–97, *88*, *89*,
   103
Lewis, Irene 102
literary criticism 7, 13, 64, 77
literary managers 8
Literary Managers and Dramaturgs of
   the Americas (L.M.D.A.) 77
logos 69–70
Lupa, Krystian 98

Mabou Mines xii, 4
Magruder, James 102
Marthaler, Christoph 98
Marx, Karl 95, 96
mathema 58
McHugh, Heather, *Not a Prayer* 108
medium 17; of time 18–19
Method acting 61–62
Meyerhold, Vsevolod 62
Michelangelo: "Captive Slaves" 15–16,
   16; *David 15*, 15–17; poetry 15–16
Miller, Arthur xiii
mimesis 21, 59; *mimesis praxeos* 49–50
Mnouchkine, Ariane 98
Molière xii, xiii, 91

Molina, Tirso de xiii
motivations 61, 76
movements 54–55
Müller, Heiner, *CIVIL warS*, "Cologne
   Section" (and Robert Wilson) 40, 80,
   96; *Alcestis* 40; *Quartet* 40

narrative 81, 87
Naturalism 62

objectives 61
opsis 5; *see also* spectacle
orexis 56
Ouspenskaya, Maria 49

painting xiii–xiv
Papp, Joe xii
pathos 57–58
performance 14; as term 6
performance events 3, 24, 34–35
Picasso, Pablo xiv, 65
Pirandello, Luigi, *Six Characters in
   Search of an Author* 65
Plautus xiii, 91
playmaking ix–x
playscripts: acting edition 100–101;
   first readings of 79–80; new play
   development 2, 8, 101, 108–109
playwrights 76, 88, 106; action of
   64–65, 102–103; dramaturgy
   principles for 108–109; as term 2
plot xv, 5–6, 19, 22, 34, 51, 54; and
   story, distinction between 17, 28, 80,
   81–87, *85*
plot-bead diagrams ix; beginnings 23;
   in full dramaturgical workup 75–76;
   hinges between beads 31, 91–94;
   overview 3–4, *4*, 24–26, *25*; for
   playwrights 108–109; Wuhan
   chicken analogy 26–28; *The Bald
   Soprano*, Eugène Ionesco 84–87, *85*;
   Einstein on the Beach, Robert
   Wilson 34–41, *37*, *38*; *Julius Caesar*,
   William Shakespeare 28–34, *29*, *33*,
   45–46; *Minna von Barnhelm*,
   Gotthold Ephraim Lessing 87–93,
   88, *89*; *Rough for Theatre II*, Samuel
   Beckett 41–47, *42*
poetry x, 14
poiesis 59, 64, 102

Pollock, Jackson xiv
postdramatic xi–xii, xiii, 4, 86
practice x–xi
praxis 9, 5, 47, 49–51, 55, 65, 102; *see also* action
presentational theatre xiii–xv, 6, 64–65
previews 79, 104–105
process 78–101; artistic freedom and copyright 99–102; prologue/overview 78–79; (1) reading the play 79–80; (2) gist/backstory and plot 80–87, *85*; (3) plot-bead diagrams (script breakdown and analysis) 87, *88, 89*; (4) sources outside the play 93–97; (5) the "take" on the play 97–100; (6) the acting edition 100–101; (7) rehearsal work/action analysis 102–103; (8) disseminating dramaturgical information 103–104; (9) tech and previews 104–105; (10) archiving production materials 105
producers 12n1
production dramaturgy 8–12, 72–107; blueprint for 72–73; disseminating information 103–104; full dramaturgical workup 75–78; making a difference 106–107; skills needed for 73–74; structural conflicts of 9–12; *see also* process
production history 77, 97–100
production week/tech 104–105
prologue/overview 78–79
psyche 51, 54–56, 59–60, 65–66; in relation to *soma* 66
Public Theater xii
purpose 52

Racine, Jean xiii
Rapoport, I.M. 51
Realism 9, xi, xiii–xiv, 5, 6, 53, 61–62
rehearsal work 102–103
representational theatre xiii–xv, 5, 6, 64
research 76–78; *see also* context
rituals xv; of beginning and end 22–24
Rochaix, François 98, 102
Ronconi, Luca 98
Rostand, Edmond xii
Rothko, Mark xiv
rules xi–xii

Saint Mark's Church-in-the-Bowery xii
Scarry, Elaine, *Dreaming by the Book* 108, 109
scenes 25–26, 52, 56–57, 62, 64, 92; in Shakespeare 28, 32
Schiller, Friedrich xiii
script doctors 1
scripts *see* playscripts
Self 65–66
sequence charts 35
Serban, Andrei 98
setting 5
Shakespeare, William xiii, 83; *Hamlet* 57, 98; *Julius Caesar* 28–34, *29, 33*, 45–46; *Measure for Measure* 43
Shepard, Sam xiii
soma 66
Sophocles xiii; *Oedipus Tyrannos* 81–82
Souter, Camille xiv
spectacle 5–6, 13–14
speech 47, 60
spheres of action 65–69, *67*
Stanislavski, Konstantin 7, 10, 51, 60–61, 65, 106; legacy 61–63; *An Actor Prepares* 26–27, 63; *Creating a Role* 10
Stanislavski System 26, 49–50, 61–62, 66, 103
Stein, Peter 98
Stewart, Ellen xii
story 4, 14, 27, 34; and plot, distinction between 17, 28, 80, 81–87, *85*
storyboard sketches *38*, 38–39
Strehler, Giorgio 98
Strindberg, August xiii
style 5, 84
subtext 60–61
Sutton, Sheryl 37
Szell, George 24

tableaux 42–43
technique x
tech/production week 104–105
tempo 3, 17, 20, 32
Terence xiii
text issues 76
Théâtre du Soleil 98
Théâtre National Populaire xii
Theatre of the Absurd 84

theatres *see* spheres of action
Theatre Workshop 51
theatricality 9–10
theme 39–40, 93
time xv, 3–4, 17, 90; aesthetic scale
    21–22; duration 19–22, 24; faculty
    18; as medium of the theatre 18–19;
    rituals of beginnings and endings
    22–24; units of 17, 19–20; *see also*
    plot-bead diagrams
tragedy xiv, 50
translation 8, 76, 100, 101

unity, aesthetic 21–22, 50–51, 90, 102,
    109

Vakhtangov, Eugene 62
van Itallie, Jean-Claude xii

Variety xi
Vega, Lope de xiii
verisimilitude xiv
Villon, François xii
visuality 5

Warner, Deborah 98
Warrilow, David 40
Wilson, Robert xii, 4, 5–6, 19, 63, 86,
    98; *CIVIL warS*, "Cologne Section"
    (and Heiner Müller) 40, 80, 96;
    Einstein on the Beach xiii, 34–40,
    37, *38*; *The Golden Windows* 40; *KA
    Mountain* 22; knee plays analogy 27;
    When We Dead Awaken 40–41
Wooster Group, The 4

Zigler, Scott 103

Printed in the United States
by Baker & Taylor Publisher Services